D0466440

Bowhunting Essentials

Hunting Wisdom Library™

MINNETONKA, MINNESOTA

About the Author

An avid outdoorsman, Bob Robb has written articles and taken photographs that have appeared regularly in almost all the major outdoor magazines for nearly two decades. The first editor of *Petersen's Bowhunting*, Bob is a former editor for both *Western Outdoor News* and *Fishing & Hunting News*, as well as a former senior staff editor for *Petersen's Hunting*. His bowhunting adventures have taken him to five continents as well as all across the United States and Canada. Bob is a member of the North American Hunting Club's Bowhunting Advisory Council and writes "Out West," a regular column for *North American Hunter* magazine.

BOWHUNTING ESSENTIALS

Mike Vail
Vice President, Product Marketing and Business Development

Tom Carpenter
Director of Book Development

Dan Kennedy
Book Production Manager
Photo Editor

Heather Koshiol
Book Development Coordinator

Beowulf Ltd.
Book Design and Production

Phil Aarrestad
Photographer

Doug Deutsher
Photographer

John Keenan
Photo Assistant/Coordinator

Ron Essex
Photo Assistant

PHOTO CREDITS
Charles Alsheimer: 15, 77, 108–109, 118, 119 (top), 120 (bottom), 133, 134, 136 (top), 140 (top), 151; Bill Buckley/The Green Agency: 10, 29 (top), 31, 36 (top), 47, 78, 162; Donald Jones: 6–7, 12, 62, 82, 121, 130, 135, 138–139, 141 (left), 143 (right), 148, 154–155, 156; Lance Krueger: 4, 13, 16 (bottom), 33 (top), 36 (bottom), 39, 110, 118 (bottom left and right), 119 (both), 125, 127 (bottom left), 137, 143 (bottom), 146 (top left), 147 (left), 163, 164–165, 166, 168, 170; Lee Lakosky, 146 (right); Bill Marchel: cover onlay, 131, 145, 167; Ian McMurchy, 116; Bob Robb: 2, 35, 46, 114, 128–129, 143 (top), 158; Tom Teitz: 1, 11 (bottom), 124, 132 (top),160, 161; Bill Vaznis/The Green Agency: 61, 123; Bill Vaznis: 11 (top), 16, 122. Remaining photographs property of NAHC: 5, 37, 120 (top), 140 (bottom), 141 (right), 142 (all), 144, 146 (bottom), 147 (right), 152, 157.

SPECIAL THANKS TO:
Barrie Archery, Blueridge, Burger Brothers, Cabin Fever, Compound Doctor, Doskocil Manufact-uring, Easton, The Footed Shaft, Golden Eagle, Golden Key Futura, Inc., Dave Maas, Matthews, McKenzie Targets, New Archery Products, Old Man Treestands, Pro Release Inc., PSE, Scent-Lok, Schaffer Performance Archery, Truball

3 4 5 6 7 8 9 / 03 02 01

ISBN 1-58159-068-7

North American Hunting Club
12301 Whitewater Drive
Minnetonka, Minnesota 55343
www.huntingclub.com

Table of Contents

Foreword

For years, the North American Hunting Club has worked diligently with the Archery Manufacturers and Merchants Organization in an effort aimed at bringing more people into bowhunting. One of the primary issues we've addressed has been mentoring. That's simply another word for teaching. Most people who've never tried bowhunting say that their primary obstacle is that they know of no one to show them how.

In your hands you hold a hammer to knock down any obstacle that stands in your way of enjoying the bowhunting tradition. In Bob Robb, you have an exceptional teacher who will take you every step of the way and instruct in plain terms that both the novice and veteran bowhunter will appreciate.

When I took up bowhunting two decades ago, I found my mentor under the Christmas tree. It was Fred Bear and his book called *The Archer's Bible*. Looking back, I don't know what I would have done without it. In fact, it's no exaggeration to say that I might not be a bowhunter today if it were not for Fred's help. My dad hunted, but not with a bow. I had a couple of friends who bowhunted, but they were learning the ropes just as I was. When I encountered a problem at the practice range or in the deer woods, I'd find the pertinent chapter in Fred's book, and he'd explain what was going on. In the fall of my 16th year, Fred's words burned to memory, I killed my first deer with a bow. And I became a bowhunter … forever.

Today much of Fred's book is long out of date, but it maintains its place on my shelf within arm's reach as I write this. Next to it, I will place this book. Though I've walked for 20 years in a bowhunter's boots, this book has offered enough insights and valuable reminders that I consider it as important as a perfect arrow. And if I were back there at the Christmas tree as an 11-year-old with dreams of big whitetails dancing in my head, I can't imagine a finer gift than this volume.

As a North American Hunting Club member, you know Bob Robb. You know him by the columns and feature articles he pens for *North American Hunter* magazine. I've had the good fortune to get to know him beyond our working relationship as writer and editor. We've hunted together for Sitka black-tailed deer on Kodiak Island, Alaska, and shared a November deer camp in Wisconsin. When some of this book strikes you as incredibly meticulous, it's because that is how Bob is. When other parts of this book surprise you with straightforwardness, it is because Bob tells it no other way. Though it is an overused cliché, it fits Bob Robb to a tee: When it comes to bowhunting, he's "been there, done that."

We North American Hunting Club members are fortunate to have the chance in this book to prepare and hunt along with him. Enjoy your bowhunting adventures.

Gregg

Gregg Gutschow
Managing Editor, *North American Hunter*

INTRODUCTION

*I*n hunting, I call my guns my "erasers." If I make a mistake and spook an animal when hunting with a firearm, it's generally not a big deal. The power and range of a firearm "erases" those mistakes. I know that when I'm gun hunting, most of the time if I can just see my quarry, it's mine.

That's one of the great allures of bowhunting: You have no eraser.

Make a bowhunting mistake, and the party's over. You can't shoot a spooked deer as it bounds off through the woods. A second shot at an animal is as rare as a four-leaf clover. If you can't get close enough, if you forget one little detail, it can mean another day of frustration and denial. The "If only…" stories are never-ending.

That's why I love it so.

Bowhunting is an up-close-and-personal affair with the woods and its wildlife. You have to be able to get close enough to smell the animal's breath to have any chance at success. Even then a shot is not guaranteed. The animal has to be calm and positioned right—with no obstructions between its chest and your arrow. Being this close has a way of destroying even the most experienced bowhunter's nerves. You have to be able to keep your cool to make the shot when the time comes.

Bowhunting is very much about becoming intimate with your equipment. There are no shortcuts to successful bow shooting. You have to pay your dues, selecting a matched bow-and-arrow setup and tuning it until broadhead-tipped arrows fly like darts. Then you must consistently practice your shooting skills until you can place your shafts where you want them, time after time. This doesn't happen by osmosis, only through dedication and hard work.

Successful bowhunters must also become highly skilled woodsmen and women. This doesn't happen by itself either. Yet in sharpening their skills, bowhunters begin to see, hear and smell things gun hunters never experience. Because by its very nature bowhunting is not a spectator sport, you're best off by yourself, with the day's outcome resting on your skills alone. In bowhunting camp, the humbling near-success stories can fill the night, creating an unparalleled camaraderie among hunters.

I am a bowhunting addict. For me, there is no cure and that's the way I like it. Try it sometime and you'll see what I mean.

— Bob Robb

Chapter 1

CHOOSING A HUNTING BOW

*H*ere's one thing you learn right off the bat: Bowhunting is an individual sport. A bowhunter is best suited to being alone in the woods, making or breaking the day's success on the merits of skill, preparation and luck.

Choosing a hunting bow is also an individual activity. Just because a well-known bowhunting personality like Chuck Adams, Ted Nugent or Myles Keller uses a particular brand and type of bow doesn't mean it's the right one for you. Simply purchasing that specific make and model—though their bows are probably well-made, high-performance tools that work well—won't necessarily make you an overnight success. That bow may even turn out to be one that, for whatever reason, you are not able to shoot particularly well.

I tell people that choosing a new bow is a lot like finding a new place to go hunting. The folks who spend the most time researching new areas, talking to people about them, then scouting the terrain before their hunt begins are the ones who consistently experience the most success. The same goes for bow shopping. Look around. Read all the literature, including reports in *North American Hunter* and bowhunting magazines. Talk to people—your hunting buddies or people you meet on the local target range or in the pro shop. Ask your resident archery pro shop owner what he recommends. By all means, shoot as many new makes and models as you can in the shop. Take your time. To a large degree, the success and enjoyment of your future bowhunting trips depends on this decision, so don't rush.

Pretty soon you'll find a bow that just feels right to you. The grip snuggles comfortably into your hand. It's smooth to draw, easy to hold at full draw and just feels right when you drop the string. It's made by a reputable manufacturer and backed by a solid warranty. Then, and only then, should you reach for your wallet.

A good friend once shared with me the analogy that selecting a hunting bow is like choosing a spouse. There are lots of good ones out there; you just have to search until you find the one you like best. Whether you're a traditional archer seeking a new recurve or longbow, or a more modern bowhunter searching for the latest in compound bow technology, first and foremost, listen to your heart.

After all, the only person you need to please in bowhunting is yourself.

TRADITIONAL BOWS

Many archers of my generation got their first taste of bows and arrows as youngsters watching Robin Hood and his merry band make fools of the Sheriff of Nottingham on television. I was fascinated by the way Robin made his arrows fly like medieval laser beams with his simple longbow and wooden shafts fletched with oversized feathers. He made it look so easy, so fun, and so doggone manly, I just had to have a bow of my own.

I drove my mom crazy with my little fiberglass kid's bow, shooting crooked shafts with their rubber cup tips at the garage door or at simple targets made from old pieces of cardboard. Pity the poor kitty that came within range! But soon I moved on to other things, like baseball, forgetting about my favorite childhood toy, and it wasn't until I went away to college that I once again took up the bow and arrow.

This time it was a classic Kodiak take-down recurve bow, a tool with which I took my first archery deer after three years of futility. That was in the mid-1970s, when the compound bow was still very much in its infancy and a neophyte like me was convinced that all that gadgetry on a bow would never work.

Today, of course, the vast majority of bowhunters choose modern equipment centered around a compound bow. Why? Because compound bows are much easier to shoot accurately and have a greater effective range and shorter learning curve for the average bowhunter than traditional bows. That does not mean that traditional tackle—the term commonly used to refer to recurves and longbows—has gone the way of the dinosaur.

Entering the 21st century, a small cadre of bowhunters and target archers have gone back to the future, spending their time afield with a well-made, modern version of these wheelless bows. Commonly, these archers have a fair amount of experience with compound bows and modern accessories. Mesmerized by the beauty of a wooden bow uncluttered by cables, wheels and high-tech sights, they have become traditional archers to recapture simplicity. These archers relish the challenge that short-range archery equipment gives them. It is a way to step back in time, forsaking a more modern compound bow that comes too close to the hustle and bustle of their daily lives. It brings them an inner peace and satisfaction they can get in no other way.

But before you get caught up in the nostalgia of traditional tackle, be forewarned that recurves and longbows are much more difficult to shoot than compound bows. They have no "let-off," which means that when you draw 50 pounds of weight on your fingers at full draw with a traditional

Making the shot instinctively brings tradition back to the hunt.

bow, you hold the full 50 pounds—not the 17.5 pounds you'd be holding if you were using a compound bow with 65 percent let-off. And most traditional bows are shot "instinctively," with no sights to help you aim. Practicing regularly with traditional bows takes a time commitment far beyond that of a compound for you to become proficient—and stay that way.

RECURVE BOWS

A recurve bow is so called because its limbs curve back toward the front of the bow. A longbow—the type of bow Robin Hood used—has limbs that curve gently back to the string. Most traditional archers today choose recurve bows because they are the easier of the two to shoot well. And their handles more closely resemble those of a compound bow, with which virtually all contemporary archers are already familiar.

Traditional recurve bow.

Due to their limb design, modern recurve bows shoot a relatively quick arrow and produce more raw arrow speed than a comparable longbow. Most modern recurves offer varying riser (handle) lengths that are designed to fit comfortably in the palm of your hand.

A wide variety of overall bow lengths are available, generally running from 46 to 72 inches, with the most popular lengths being 60 to 64 inches. The length recurve you need is directly related to your draw length. Generally speaking, shooters with a draw length of 28 to 29 inches choose a bow between 60 and 62 inches in length, while shooters with a draw length of 29 to 30 inches choose a bow between 62 and 64 inches in length.

There are two basic types of recurve bow designs: one-piece and take-down. A one-piece bow is just that—a bow with both limbs integrated into the riser. A take-down bow is built from three pieces—the riser and two limbs that can be easily removed.

While one-piece bows are lightweight and unmatched in balance, the two-piece models are much more versatile. Not only can the limbs be removed for ease of storage and transport, but they can be replaced with limbs that are longer or shorter, heavier or lighter... in effect allowing you to create a whole new bow just by swapping limbs. Most recurve limbs are made from laminated wood and fiberglass, and the risers are made from laminated wood or, in some cases, machined aluminum.

When selecting a recurve, choose one with a draw weight that you can easily draw and shoot. A bow with a draw weight of more than 50 pounds is very difficult for most people to shoot well. Choosing a recurve with a draw weight that is too heavy is the absolute worst thing you can do when you're trying to learn proper shooting techniques.

LONGBOWS

The most primitive of hunting bows, the longbow doesn't shoot as fast an arrow as a recurve, its bare-bones handle can be difficult to hold properly and the shock delivered through the handle at the shot can be unnerving. Yet it is precisely this primitive nature that draws a small segment of today's bowhunting population to them.

Like the recurve, the modern longbow is usually built with modern materials, particularly fiberglass, which is used in laminating the limbs. But there is a longbow made from a single piece of wood—called the "self" bow—which has drawn a small proportion of archers into its camp. And while almost all longbows are of one-piece design, a few take-down longbows are available as well.

Longbows are longer than comparable recurves because of the performance characteristics of the limbs. Shooters with a draw length of 27 to 29 inches usually choose longbows with an overall length of 66 inches.

The longbow is the least efficient of all hunting bows, meaning it produces the slowest overall raw arrow speed when compared to compound and recurve bows. Yet when choosing a longbow, you don't try to overcompensate by choosing a bow

Traditional longbow.

with too high a draw weight. As is the case with all bows, you guarantee mediocre shooting by selecting a bow with a draw weight too heavy for you to shoot smoothly and comfortably.

BOWHUNTING WITH TRADITIONAL TACKLE

Don't think that choosing a traditional bow limits your chances of harvesting game. Each fall, traditional archers take hundreds of deer and successfully pursue other game. For example, my friend G. Fred Asbell, one of the founders of *Bowhunter* magazine and an authority on instinctive shooting, spent two weeks in the rugged Chugach Mountains of Alaska under adverse weather conditions yet came away with a beautiful Dall sheep ram taken with traditional tackle.

Just like hunting with a modern compound, the secret to success with traditional tackle is, first and foremost, to choose a bow that fits you properly and that you can draw smoothly and comfortably. Then you must undertake a diligent program of practice until you become a proficient shot and learn what your personal maximum effective shooting range is. Finally, use your own skill as a guideline and organize your hunting trip in such a manner that you try to put yourself into position to get a shot close enough that you are comfortable with it.

Bowhunting with traditional tackle is not for everyone. But for many who have made the switch from a modern, bells-and-whistles compound to the simplicity of a recurve or longbow, time afield is about much more than maximizing their chances at putting meat in the pot. It's about inner peace and self-satisfaction.

In the final analysis, isn't that what it's all about?

Instinctive shooting takes hours of dedicated practice ... all in anticipation of that one fleeting, magical moment.

THE MODERN COMPOUND BOW

rest and fiber-optic bow sight—screams modern-day technology. Yet this fact connects the two types: Both are short-range tools that force the hunter to get extremely close to game without being detected, to make a killing shot possible.

The advantage of the compound bow over a recurve or longbow lies in the compound's system of round or eccentric wheels and cables that work together as the bowstring is pulled back to reduce a given bow's "holding weight" well below its listed "draw weight." Here's how it works.

When the traditional archer draws the bowstring back, the bow reaches its peak draw weight—the heaviest amount of pressure needed to draw the string back—at full draw. There the archer must hold that pressure on his or her fingers until he or she is ready to release the arrow. Let's say that's 70 pounds. It takes a lot of strength to hold that much weight for any length of time, which is one reason traditional archers who shoot instinctively draw and release the arrow in one fluid motion that doesn't require them to hold the bow at full draw for more than a few seconds.

With a compound bow, the archer has a distinct mechanical advantage provided by the bow's wheels and cables. A compound bow with a peak draw weight of the same 70 pounds and a let-off of

*T*he invention and successful marketing of the compound bow changed the face of bowhunting forever. There is little doubt that without the compound bow—which made it easier than ever for the novice to learn quickly how to shoot a bow accurately—bowhunting would not be nearly as popular as it is today.

While both traditional and compound bows use limbs attached to a handle or riser and a bowstring to propel an arrow shaft forward, the differences between the two are dramatic. The sleek, uncluttered lines of traditional equipment speak volumes on old-school simplicity and tradition. On the other hand, a compound bow—with its system of cables and wheels and adorned with accessories like a stabilizer, wrist strap, multiposition arrow

65 percent—a common let-off for today's bows—also forces the shooter to put 70 pounds of pressure on his fingers as the bow is drawn back to about the halfway point. But thanks to the mechanical advantage provided by the bow's pulley system, that 70-pound peak weight is reduced as the shooter continues to pull the bowstring all the way back to full draw, where he has to hold only 35 percent of the bow's peak draw weight on his fingers until the time of release: that's just 24.5 pounds of pressure! This allows the archer to aim longer at the target without muscle fatigue. Longer aim time facilitates the use of a bow sight, which means you'll shoot a more accurate arrow.

In the early days of compound bows, the common let-off was about 50 percent. Today, let-offs commonly fall between 65 and 85 percent. Bows with high let-off are increasingly popular despite the fact that, for entry into their record book, the Pope and Young Club will not recognize animals taken with bows with a let-off of more than 65 percent.

COMPOUND BOW POWER

One common misconception among compound bow shooters is that their bows have an inordinate amount of "power" to drive their arrow shafts deeply into the target. For many years, a bow's draw weight was the common way many archers determined power potential. Simply put, if your bow had a peak draw weight of 70 pounds, and mine had a peak draw weight of only 60 pounds, your bow had more power.

Maybe. And maybe not. Many more factors go to work here than just draw weight: Differences in draw length, bow style and the power stroke of different bow designs also contribute. Today, thanks to variations in basic bow design, it is possible for a particular bow with a draw weight of 60 pounds to shoot arrows of equal weight and length with more kinetic energy (KE) than a bow with an 80-pound draw weight.

To understand how this can be, you must first understand the basics of how a bow works.

When you draw the bowstring back, you exert

"Loaded" limbs store the kinetic energy needed to penetrate large animals.

effort. This energy is transferred to and stored in the bow's bent limbs. When you release the string, most of this stored energy—but not all—transfers to the arrow shaft, which uses the energy to fly through the air and penetrate the target. Leaving the bow, the arrow converts the stored energy into KE, which is defined as the energy of mass in motion. Bow power is based on the fact that KE has the ability to do work; therefore, the more KE the arrow possesses, the harder it will hit and the deeper it will penetrate.

The key to bow power is having a bow that stores as much energy as possible, then delivers most of that energy to the arrow. The amount of energy transferred to the arrow is known as "bow efficiency." Most of today's compound bows deliver 70 to 80 percent of stored energy to the arrow shaft.

With compound bows of the same draw length and draw weight, the key factor in a compound bow's ability to store energy is the shape or design of the cam. For example, a round-wheel bow with a 60-pound draw weight might store 1 foot-pound (fp) of energy for every pound of draw weight, for a total of roughly 60 fp of stored energy. However,

Choosing and tuning the correct bow is as important as making a good shot. In fact, choosing, tuning and good shooting are intricately related.

this same bow with an energy wheel might store almost 1.5 fp of energy for every pound of draw weight. That would translate into nearly 90 fp of stored energy, or 33 percent more!

The bow's "power stroke"—the distance over which the bow delivers power to the arrow upon release of the string—is the other factor that affects the amount of energy a bow can store. The shooter's draw length and the bow's brace height—the distance measured between the bowstring and bow handle when the bow is in the undrawn position—are the two factors that most affect power stroke.

Brace height is a function of bow design; in general, a bow with a shorter brace height lengthens the power stroke, which in turn produces more stored energy. And a longer draw length will also produce more stored energy, simply because drawing the bowstring is what causes energy to be stored in a bow's limbs.

To determine your bow's kinetic energy, all you need are two numbers: the weight of your arrow shaft and its initial velocity. Weigh your shaft—complete with arrow point attached—on a grain scale, then shoot it through a chronograph, and you'll have what you need.

Next, plug the numbers into this formula:

$$KE = \frac{\text{arrow weight in grains} \times \text{velocity}^2}{450,240}$$

For example, a bow shooting an arrow shaft weighing 525 grains and leaving the bow at 250 feet per second (fps) has a kinetic energy of 72.88 fp of energy.

How much KE do you need for bowhunting? That depends, of course, on many things. First, no generally recognized KE minimum has been established by the various national archery and bowhunting organizations for bowhunting game animals. For deer-sized game, 35 fp—the KE generated by a bow shooting a 400-grain arrow at 200 fps—is probably enough if you place your arrow, tipped with a razor-sharp broadhead, in the animal's vitals at short range. Larger game, like elk and bears, require more KE to get the job done efficiently. The secret is to employ an efficient bow that you can draw comfortably and shoot accurately, then place the shaft into the animal's vitals. Even the most powerful bow in the world won't give you an edge if you can't shoot it with consistent accuracy.

Shooting a bow you're comfortable with will make you a better shooter, period.

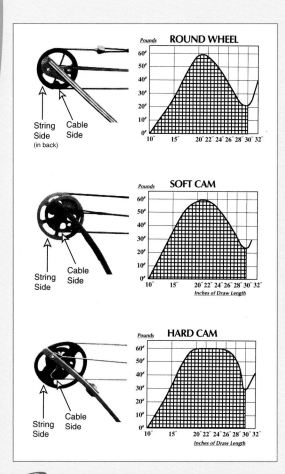

recurves and longbows plot the simplest curves because they build up their poundage at a steady rate. Their design is such that the farther back the bowstring is pulled, the more poundage the bow accumulates, and thus the more energy the bow's limbs store.

Initially, all compound bows were made with wheels that were round on both the string side and cable side of the wheel. Today, bow designers regularly modify the shape on one or both sides to improve performance.

Bows with a true round wheel design, which are tough to find today, store the least amount of energy of the three basic wheel types. Most bows are currently manufactured with soft cams, which feature a moderating shape on the wheel's string side and a more oblique, egg-shaped design on the wheel's cable side. This design gives the archer a good balance between the smooth drawing characteristics of pure round wheels and the speed of radical cam designs. The third design type, called hard cam or speed cam, stores the maximum amount of energy and thus produces the fastest arrow flight. These cams—which feature a radically egg-shaped surface on the wheel's cable side— are the toughest to draw and shoot smoothly.

As the top of the curve widens, the amount of energy under the curve increases and the back side of the curve becomes steeper. The angle of the slope where the poundage drops off shows the speed at which the bow's energy is transferred to the arrow when the string is released. In other words, the steeper the back slope, the more rapidly the bow transfers the energy to the arrow.

While it is impossible to plot your own bow's force draw curve without some special equipment, bow manufacturers do it all the time. You can see these recommendations in arrow selection charts, which recommend using a stiffer-spined arrow for bows using more radical cam designs; this compensates for the increased energy transfer and potential arrow speed these designs produce.

The way in which different bows store and release energy is the basis for their performance differences, which are measured with what is known as the "force draw curve." The shape of the force draw curve shows how each bow stores energy when you draw the string and how this energy is transferred to the arrow when you released the string. On a compound bow, the design of the wheel or cam largely determines the shape of the force draw curve. The total area "under the curve" represents the total amount of energy stored.

On a force draw curve chart, the numbers on the left side represent the bow's poundage, or draw weight. The numbers on the bottom of the chart represent the bow's draw length in inches. As you can see from the accompanying chart,

CHOOSING A COMPOUND BOW

The Archery Manufacturer's and Merchant's Association (AMO) defines draw length as "the distance at full draw from the nocking point to a point 1³/₄ inches beyond the pivot point of the grip." Most bowhunters start off with a bow set at a draw length that's too long for them. For bowhunting, a good rule of thumb is to set the bow's draw length slightly on the short side, generally by ¹/₄ to ¹/₂ inch.

First, you must measure your true draw length. Here's the best way. Pull a light-draw-weight bow to full draw with a long arrow on the bowstring, anchor it using the same anchor point you'll use when shooting, and have a friend mark the shaft at the midpoint of the bow handle, where the arrow rest hole has been drilled. (Archery pro shops have a special arrow for this purpose.) Next, measure the shaft from that mark to the string groove on the arrow's nock, add 1³/₄ inches, and that's your draw length as specified by industry standards. Remember: Draw length is not arrow length. Usually you'll shoot arrows that are a bit longer or shorter than your

Walk into any well-stocked archery pro shop, peruse the pages of one of today's bowhunting magazines or look over a mail-order archery catalog. You'll see why many novice archers and bowhunters quickly become confused. It is easy to get "sensory overload" as you look over the seemingly endless array of compound bows and accessories. Which bow is best for you, and what accessories will help complete your setup?

No one can tell you what you need. After all, selecting a compound bow is as much a function of personal taste as it is a scientific endeavor. The secret is choosing a bow that pleases you and, at the same time, is able to perform reliably for many years.

Before we discuss the pros and cons of various compound bow features, you must first determine two key personal physical characteristics: your draw length and draw weight.

DETERMINING DRAW LENGTH

Choosing a compound bow with exactly the right draw length is critical to accurate shooting.

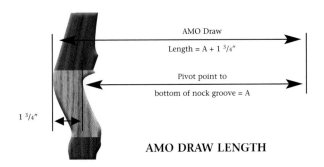

How to measure draw length.

true draw length. We'll talk more about this later.

Your draw length will vary according to whether you shoot with a release aid or your fingers, and it can change slightly depending on the type and model of bow you shoot and the type of arrow rest employed. You'll also find that your draw length may change over time as you become more comfortable shooting compound bows in general. Virtually all modern compound bows come with variable draw length settings, making it easy to set the bow to your exact measurements.

DETERMINING DRAW WEIGHT

AMO defines draw weight as "the maximum level of force needed to draw the bow back to the full or cocked position." Most compound bows have draw weight ranges that can be adjusted 10 to 15 pounds. The two most common bows have draw weights of 55 to 70 pounds and 65 to 80 pounds.

Because of today's efficient compound bows, it isn't necessary to pull an inordinate amount of draw weight to produce reasonably fast arrow flight and enough kinetic energy for almost all bowhunting situations. Today many archers pull bows with draw weights of just 55 to 65 pounds, and their bows produce plenty of raw arrow speed for most bowhunting situations. When you pull more draw weight than you can comfortably handle, you sacrifice bow control, which is the real key to accurate shooting.

To measure your correct draw weight, take these simple tests. Standing flat-footed, hold the bow at arm's length and pull it back. If you have to "cheat"—lift the bow up above your head—to achieve full draw, the draw weight is too heavy. Next, do the same thing from a seated position, as if you were sitting in a treestand. Finally, do it from a kneeling position. Being able to draw your bow—even from weird angles—with a minimum of movement is important when bowhunting. Extra body movement can spook an animal, so the less movement, the better. Remember that the longer you shoot your bow, the stronger your bow-pulling muscles will get, which will allow you to increase your draw weight comfortably.

GETTING DOWN TO BUSINESS

Once you've found your draw length and draw weight, it's time to look at bows. At first glance, modern compounds may all look alike. But subtle differences in basic design will affect both the bow's performance and whether or not you'll personally like it. To make a smart buying decision, you must first understand the basics about a compound bow's different components and how they affect performance.

WHEELS & CAMS

There are three basic traditional compound bow wheel designs. Each offers advantages and disadvantages for the bowhunter.

Round wheels are smooth to draw, very quiet and inherently accurate. However, round wheels are the slowest of the three basic designs, one reason they've fallen out of favor with today's bowhunters. Soft cams feature part of the design as a roundish wheel and part as an egg-shaped cam. This design, which produces a smoothness

Use the scale at an archery shop to determine an actual, accurate draw weight for your bow.

Choosing a Hunting Bow

From left: Hard, soft and round cams.

and reliability comparable to a round wheel but also provides increased arrow speed, is the most popular with today's bowhunters. Hard cams, or speed cams, are egg-shaped eccentrics that store the most energy of all the basic designs, thus producing the fastest arrow flight. Hard cams tend to be a bit noisy and are the most difficult design to shoot well consistently.

A fourth design of compound bow, the one-cam bow, also became a rage. One-cam bows feature an oversized energy-storing cam on the lower limb, but instead of a similar cam on top, they have a concentric wheel, called an "idler." We'll talk more about one-cam bows later on (pages 24-25).

THE RISER

A bow's riser, commonly referred to as the handle, is generally made of aluminum or magnesium. A modern riser's offset, or cutout, design makes it easier for the arrow fletching and broadhead blades to clear the riser during the shot.

There are three basic handle designs: straight, reflexed and deflexed. Limb pockets are directly in line with straight handles. A deflexed handle has the limb pockets positioned slightly behind the handle. The limb pockets lie slightly in front of a reflexed handle. Generally

speaking, bows with either straight or reflexed handles have a lower brace height than bows with deflexed handles; thus they produce an inherently faster arrow. Deflexed riser bows, on the other hand, are usually a bit more forgiving to shoot.

The most important thing a bow handle can do for you is offer a grip that feels comfortable in your hand. Some shooters will sand or file a grip down a bit to fit their hand more precisely. Others will add tape or premade plastic or wooden grips to alter the feel. When shopping for a new bow, pick up several and see how each feels. The one that feels best is generally the bow you'll shoot best.

BOW LIMBS

Compound bow limbs come in both straight and recurve designs. Both work equally well, the only difference being how you like their looks. There are two basic limb materials used today: laminated wood and fiberglass. Fiberglass limbs

Risers differ in design, but choosing one is simple: The comfortable one is probably the right one for you.

Split limb (left) vs. solid limb.

are generally more dependable and trouble-free, and produce top-end performance. But wood limbs are excellent too and weigh a bit less. You can't go wrong with either material.

For many years, all bow limbs were solid. Today, many manufacturers offer some compound bows with split limbs: limbs with the center section of both the upper and lower limbs removed, creating a slightly lighter-weight bow than a solid-limb bow. Some manufacturers claim that split limbs also reduce noise and increase arrow speed a bit. Others say that split-limb bows are less reliable than solid-limb bows, more difficult to tune and not as consistent. I've shot both, and both have worked well for me.

STRINGS & CABLES

Dacron was the material of choice for bow-strings in early compound bows, while cable systems consisted of metal. Way back in 1985, Brownell & Co. introduced a synthetic material called Fast Flight (technically called "Spectra"), which is stronger and stretches less. Today most bow companies offer complete Fast Flight string and cable systems. Another string material, Vectran, does not stretch or creep over time, as Fast Flight will; however, it is a bit less tolerant of abrasion. And a combination of Fast Flight and Vectran, called S4, is a durable, low-stretch string and cable material.

Compound bows also utilize a cable guard, which holds the cable to the side of the bowstring and prevents fletch contact during the shot. Cable guards are placed either above or below the arrow nock, depending on bow design.

BOW LENGTH

Overall bow length is an important perform-ance factor. Bows with a shorter axle-to-axle length generally produce more raw arrow speed than longer bows. (The axle is the rod that holds the wheel into the end of the bow limb.) Bows with axle-to-axle lengths between 37 and 41 inch-es are the most popular. Besides increased arrow speed, shorter bows lend themselves to the use of some sort of mechanical release aid, which is how the majority of contemporary archers shoot, instead of a fingers release. For fingers shooters, longer bows between 42 and 44 inches in length are better because they reduce the amount of "fin-ger pinch." Shorter bows are also easier to maneu-ver in the field—among the limbs and branches encountered while in a treestand and through brush while hunting on the ground.

A cable guard attaches to your cable and slides, allowing the arrow's fletches to clear as the arrow leaves the string.

New compounds have become smaller, lighter and faster.

you to shoot shorter—and therefore lighter—arrows. In years past, the most popular way bowhunters achieved more raw arrow speed was by using some sort of overdraw. But overdraws have their problems, the biggest being that they make it imperative for the archer to maintain excellent shooting form throughout the shot sequence to avoid torque that will throw the shaft off-target. The longer the overdraw, the more exaggerated this problem can become.

With today's efficient, high-performance compound bows, using an overdraw isn't really necessary. Though they are an advantage for shooters with extremely long arms, for most of us, it's better to sacrifice a few feet per second of arrow speed to eliminate the shooting problems an overdraw can produce.

There is a downside to shorter bows: They are more subject to the problems of hand torque on the riser during the shot, which can result in poor accuracy. Unless you're an expert shooter, it's best to start out with a bow that's longer than 38 inches.

OVERDRAWS

An overdraw is an arrow rest bracket that extends about 6 inches behind the riser, allowing

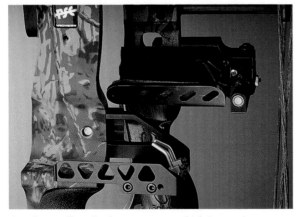

Overdraws allow for shorter arrows, which in turn increases arrow speed.

STABILIZERS

Stabilizers—elongated metal bars that screw into the front of the riser—help overcome a bow's tendency to "jump" forward at the shot. How? They reduce hand torque and help counterbalance the bow's rearward weight. The added weight of a stabilizer also helps you to steady the bow as you aim and release. Plus, the stabilizer helps reduce vibration and noise during the shot.

Stabilizers come in all shapes and sizes.

Inexpensive stabilizers are machined from a solid piece of metal. A bit more expensive are hydraulic stabilizers, which improve performance. Most hunting stabilizers are between 4 and 10 inches long. Adding one to a high-performance compound bow will, in most cases, help your shooting.

BUYING A HUNTING COMPOUND BOW

Today, all major bow manufacturers build excellent hunting bows backed with a solid warranty. Most also offer a full line of accessory items,

Accessory packages take the guesswork out of what you need and provide components well-matched to your bow.

including bow sights, quivers and arrow rests.

The best place to buy a new bow is from a reputable archery pro shop. Here you can examine several different models and accessory packages, as well as get expert advice on the features and benefits you'll need for the bowhunting you'll be doing. Most important, the resident pro will: help you set up your bow the right way, making sure the draw length and draw weight are correct; help you select the right arrow shafts; and help you tune your bow until it's shooting darts. The resident pro will also be there when you have problems and need a little help in working the kinks out of both your bow and your shooting form.

When choosing a new bow, the bottom line is to select the one that you like best. Simply stated, it will feel good in your hand and be comfortable to shoot. While it's smart to ask your friends their opinions, remember that you're the one whose success or failure depends on this bow.

Bowshop experts can help you pick out what you need for your bow. Trust their opinions and suggestions.

Discovering Your Dominant Eye

Before choosing any compound bow, you'll first need to discover something about yourself. That discovery will tell you whether or not you should shoot your bow right- or left-handed. Surprisingly, this has nothing to do with whether you're right- or left-handed, but whether you're right- or left-eye dominant. Normally the dominant eye is on the same side of the body as the dominant hand, but not always. Here are two ways to find out.

Hold your hands at arm's length, then form a small hole—like a telescope—with your fingers. Keep both your eyes open and center a distant object through this hole. Slowly draw your hands toward your face while staying focused on the object in the center of the hole. Your hands will naturally come back to your dominant eye.

Or point at a distant object with your arm extended fully in front of you and raised to eye level. Now close or cover your left eye, staying focused on the object with the right eye. Repeat, this time closing or covering the right eye. When you look through the dominant eye, the object will still appear to be in line with your finger. When you look through the subordinate eye, the object will appear to have shifted noticeably to the side.

THE ONE-CAM PHENOMENON

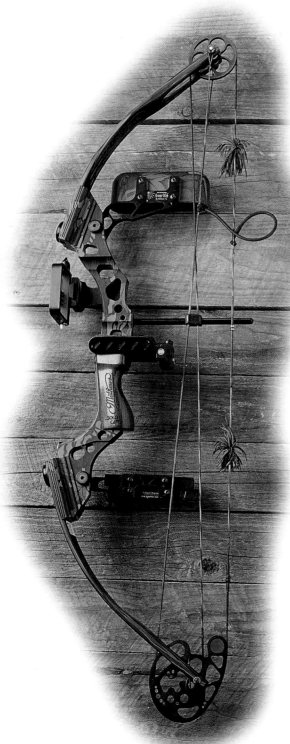

*T*raditionally designed modern compound bows have a pair of wheels (or cams) of exactly the same shape, size and design. These have generally been classified into three basic types—round wheel, soft cam and hard cam—with the more radical design of cam producing more raw arrow speed, all other things being equal.

As the buying public began demanding more efficient bows that produced faster arrow speed and flatter trajectory, manufacturers began producing more hunting bows with hard-cam designs. On the surface, this would seem like a good thing. But one must remember that, as in all things in life, nothing is free. Shooters found that hard-cam bows were generally much more sensitive to inconsistencies in shooter form and were also noisier and more difficult to keep in perfect tune than bows with softer cams. And they are harder to draw, making them better suited to advanced shooters than the average weekend bowhunter.

Enter the one-cam (also called the single-cam) design.

At first glance, having identical wheels on both limbs makes a lot of sense. This obviously facilitates the limbs working in perfect harmony as the bow is drawn and shot. If that's true, then why in the world would you want a single-cam bow, which features a roundish "idler" wheel on the upper limb and an oversized cam on the lower limb?

A LITTLE HISTORY

While bow makers have dabbled in the single-cam design for many years—the old Dynabow of the early 1970s is a prime example—it really didn't grab the market's attention until Matt McPherson introduced his single-cam design to the archery world in the spring of 1992. To say that his single-cam took the industry by storm would be a gross understatement.

"For years, all savvy engineers working on compound bow design knew that a single-cam design would be better than a two-cam design if they could make it work," McPherson recounts. "The old Dynabow had the problem of very poor nock travel, which really doomed it from the start."

"The problem we all faced was making a single-cam design that was simple because there was lots to be done to control nock travel," McPherson explained. "When it finally hit me, I wasn't really trying to design a bow. It just sort of popped into my head, more of a gift than something I really worked for. I went and built a model, and by golly, it worked. I then started my own bow manufacturing company, Mathews Archery, to build and market it."

WHY SWITCH TO A ONE-CAM BOW?

From an engineering point of view, the advantages of the single-cam to the shooter are many.

"The primary benefits of the single-cam are centered around the issue of wheel timing," describes Derek Phillips of Mathews Archery, a highly accomplished tournament archer and bowhunter. "With two-cam bows, it's very difficult to synchronize the oblong-shaped cams to roll over at exactly the same time. When they do not, the result is an inconsistency in performance. But since with a single-cam bow you have only one cam, not two, the issue of wheel timing has been eliminated altogether. That fosters consistent shot-to-shot accuracy like no other bow design on today's market."

There are other benefits as well. "The key to the success of any new product, in any field, is whether or not it will perform better than the existing product," reveals Matt McPherson, who introduced the single-cam design to the archery world almost a decade ago now. "Often, the new product will perform better, but it is also more complicated and therefore more expensive. But with the single-cam bow, it not only performs better, but it is also simpler, which makes it competitively priced with two-cam bows."

"The key to the single-cam's success is certainly wheel timing," McPherson shares, "but it's more than that. They are easier to tune and to keep in tune. They are also much more consistent shot to shot, and they have a much more solid wall at full draw than a two-cam bow; this means they are much easier to anchor and aim exactly the same every time, which helps the shooter release the arrow exactly the same every time. And as we all know, it is this kind of consistency that breeds accurate shooting." That these points are true is

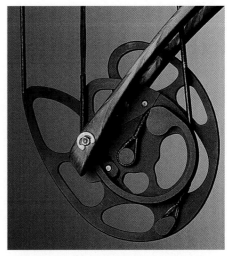

Matt McPherson, president of Matthews Archery, pioneered the one-cam bow.

underscored by the fact that the vast majority of the nation's top 3-D tournament shooters—folks who make their living shooting a bow and arrow with surgical precision—are presently shooting single-cam bows.

In all the hoopla over the single-cam bow, let's not forget the inevitable trade-offs. At first, single-cam bows were measurably slower than comparable two-cam models. "It took lots of design work, but we've solved the speed issue with current models," assures McPherson. "Today's single-cam bows are very comparable with two-cam bows in terms of raw arrow speed while retaining all their other benefits."

McPherson sold his single-cam patent to Bear/Jennings Archery while retaining some royalty rights, which means that all other manufacturers who use this new design must pay a royalty for the privilege. Still, that has not deterred other bow makers from jumping on the single-cam bandwagon. "The single-cam trend is not coming, it's here," Phillips declares. "It's just too good a design not to build and promote."

Does the rising popularity of the single-cam bow mean that traditional two-cam models are obsolete? Not on your life; those bow designs still offer the same excellent performance they always have. Manufacturers will continue to offer a wide selection of two-cam bows in the coming years. But, each year, more and more shooters are discovering the benefits of the one-cam design. When shopping for a new hunting bow, you would do well to check out one-cams before making your final decision.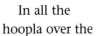

Chapter 2

ACCESSORIES FOR YOUR COMPOUND BOW

*T*hough bowhunting is a simple sport, it can rapidly become complicated when it comes time to select the right accessory items to "trick out" your new hunting compound.

As you'll quickly learn, there is much more to readying a new bow for the target range or deer woods than checking out several different makes and models, then melting down your credit card. You have to sort through a maze of different arrow rest styles and designs, and choose a bow sight that is rugged enough to withstand the hunting woods yet precise enough to foster the shooting of tight groups on the target range. Do you want a quiver that attaches to the bow or one you carry yourself? Or maybe you want one that attaches to the bow but is removed before you begin hunting? How about those little knickknacks like moleskin, string wax and an arm guard? And what the heck is a kisser button anyway?

Don't despair. Half the fun of bowhunting is in the little accessory items that can help make our shooting more accurate, our bows more reliable, our days afield more enjoyable. One of my favorite ways to spend an evening is to head down to the local archery pro shop and enter into the debate—as you'll soon learn, pro shops always have a debate of some sort going on—over the merits of this little item over that one. Which is better? Do we really need any of them? Who thought of such a stupid product in the first place? And then you go try it out, and as often as not you'll come away thinking, "You know, this really is a pretty slick little gizmo. Maybe I need one after all ..."

At the same time, don't add a million and one items that you really don't need to your bow and equipment. Most bowhunters go through an evolution that begins with needing to have one of everything ever made, and then, as they become more experienced, they remember the acronym KISS—Keep It Simple, Stupid—and begin eliminating more and more things from their list of necessary "stuff."

How do you know what you need and what you don't? Read on, and we'll help you decide.

THE MODERN ARROW REST

*T*he arrow rest is a lot like Rodney Dangerfield—it just don't get no respect. Most archers have a devil-may-care attitude about their rests, not giving them a second thought. But few accessory items are more important. Using an arrow rest that has not been designed specifically for your style of shooting and hunting, that doesn't fit precisely onto your bow or that has been built cheaply, leads to disaster.

To understand the whys and hows of modern arrow rests, it helps to understand how they have evolved over the past four decades.

ANCIENT ARROW RESTS

From the days of Robin Hood up through the early 20th century, archers shooting longbows did little more than rest their arrow shafts across the fist of their bow hand. Change occurred as the recurve bow developed in the 1950s. Recurves are built with an arrow shelf carved into the grip. Archers covered these shelves with pieces of low-pile carpet, cloth or leather. This style of shooting, called "off the shelf," was a step up in consistent accuracy.

Archers began using the first removable arrow rests sometime in the 1960s. They were little more than a horizontal plastic, hair or feather shelf for the arrow to rest upon, sometimes with a plastic or nylon side plate against which the shaft would rest. Soon a few arrow rests permitted some horizontal side plate adjustments, which greatly aided in accurate shooting at longer ranges for skilled archers. Most of these rests attached to the bow with double-backed adhesive tape. You can still find these inexpensive arrow rests today.

The Berger Button changed the face of arrow rests forever. Invented by tournament shooter Norman Pint but named for well-known competitive archer Victor Berger in the mid-1960s, this spring-loaded button cushioned the shaft as it was released to reduce side-to-side oscillation, which in turn tightened arrow groups dramatically. When used in conjunction with the popular adhesive-backed Flipper or Flipper II arrow shelf, the combination became the standard against which all other rests of the late 1960s and early 1970s were judged. Modern arrow rests featuring this general design are generically called cushion plungers.

Rare today, the springy rest—nothing more than a threaded brass barrel connected to a coiled, one-piece spring-wire plate-and-shelf unit—was a popular variation of the cushion plunger in the 1970s. Springys—horizontally adjustable—were sold in a variety of spring gauges and tension weights to accommodate different bow weights and arrow stiffnesses.

The 1980s saw the rise of the prong, or launcher-type, arrow rest. Southern Californian Fred Troncoso, a professional musician and serious tournament archer, created this design in 1967 and founded Golden Key-Futura a year later. The prong-type rest cradles the arrow shaft between

Early designs in arrow rests paved the way for today's better, more effective models.

two fingerlike prongs, requiring no side pressure from a Berger Button. "This was before release aids were around, but the prong rest worked great anyway," Troncoso remarks. "Unfortunately, no one was really interested in such a 'radical' arrow rest at that time."

Troncoso's first patented arrow rest was the Match One, patented in 1973–'74, followed by the Pace Setter Vee-launcher-type rest a year later. It wasn't until 1982–'83 that Troncoso's Vee-launcher rest first became accepted by a significant number of archers. Back then these rest types were commonly called "wrap-around" rests because the rest unit attached to the Berger Button hole tapped into the off-side of the bow's riser, then wrapped around the back side of the riser.

The evolution of the arrow rest continues today, with variations of proven rest designs and styles widespread, resulting in the largest selection of quality arrow rests in history.

TODAY'S ARROW RESTS

Before choosing an arrow rest, you should understand the basics of how arrow shafts bend, or oscillate, when released. High-speed photography shows that arrows bend a surprising amount during the shot, the amount and type of bending a direct result of both shaft stiffness and the way the shaft is released. The shaft does not

recover from this oscillation until it has traveled downrange several yards. Despite this oscillation, clearing the arrow rest—both the shaft itself and its fletching—is crucial to accurate shooting.

When you release an arrow with your fingers, it oscillates from side to side, the first large bend being away from the bow's handle. This type of release lends itself to the cushion-plunger style of arrow rest because as the shaft bends away from the bow, it also bends away from the arrow rest. Conversely, a shaft that's released with a mechanical release aid tends to bend up and down, not side to side. This lends itself to the use of a Vee-launcher or prong-type arrow rest. That's because when the bowstring is released, the shaft first takes a large upward bend away from the rest's two metal prongs.

Surveys by leading arrow rest makers indicate that 80 to 90 percent of today's archers, including both bowhunters and target shooters, use some type of release aid. That means most of them should be using the basic shoot-through, prong-type arrow rest design. To that end, the industry directs most of its arrow rest research and development efforts toward this type of rest.

But the cushion-plunger style of rest has not been forsaken completely. Fingers shooters still prefer this basic design, and a few ardent release

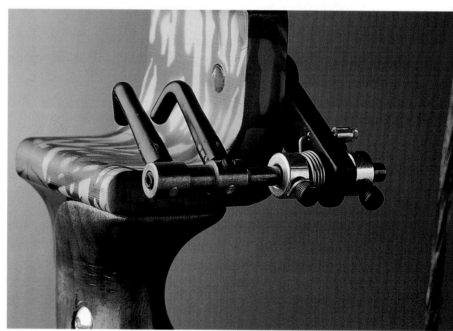
Prong arrow rests are the most popular design among today's bowhunters. Prong rests work beautifully with release aids.

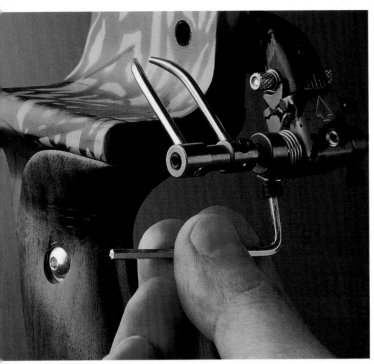

New arrow rests allow for minor adjustments and fine tuning, without moving the whole rest.

shooters use a cushion plunger that also permits some sort of downward movement at the shot by the rest arm.

DESIGN FEATURES

If you examine the many different arrow rests available today, you will find rests ranging from simple to complex. Some rests have few adjustment features, while others—notably those designed with the serious target archer in mind—have more screws and adjustment knobs than the space shuttle.

Microadjustable arrow rests are the rage today. These rests permit vertical and horizontal adjustments that can be made in minute increments, permitting precise adjustments that allow archers to tune their bows perfectly. But many of these rests ultimately disappoint bowhunters who find the complex adjustment systems difficult to work with. In addition, the many tiny adjustment screws and knobs often rattle loose or slip during hunting season, which of course destroys accuracy.

Manufacturers have taken a cue from bowhunters, who want simpler designs that require less maintenance during the course of a

hunting season. Bowhunters demand reliability but also need to be able to make both vertical and horizontal adjustments easily. The best arrow rests today are simple to set up, quick to dial in and built to last through tough field use and to hold up in extreme weather conditions.

The most complex arrow rests tend to be the Vee-launcher and shoot-through types. Cushion-plunger rests remain the most simple, although today's versions are much more complicated than Pint's first designs. With several dozen companies building and marketing arrow rests today, finding the right rest for your shooting and hunting is simply a matter of looking over several different designs, then test-driving as many as possible at your local pro shop before making a final decision.

CARBON ARROWS: A UNIQUE CHALLENGE

While aluminum arrows are still the number-one seller for both target shooting and bowhunting, each year a growing number of archers are discovering the benefits of small-diameter carbon arrow shafts. They're also discovering the challenges posed by these small-diameter shafts in terms of choosing and using an arrow rest.

Due to a carbon arrow's much smaller diameter compared to an aluminum shaft, its arrow fletches must be closer together on the shaft. Because fletch clearance is the most difficult part of achieving complete arrow rest clearance at the shot, precision in an arrow rest is necessary to allow for the small adjustments needed to achieve this clearance.

Carbon fiber is an extremely abrasive material. Shooting carbon shafts across the arrow rest leads to a high heat buildup, which rapidly destroys the rubber and/or plastic shrink tubing that's been used for many years to help silence the sound of a shaft as it is drawn and shot across the metal prongs of a shoot-through rest. Because I have not yet found a material that will withstand a couple hundred shots with carbon shafts, one season I tried removing any form of silencing material all together. My pure carbon shafts actually wore grooves in the metal prongs of my shoot-through rest! To date, no manufacturer has solved this abrasion problem; I remedy it by using stick-on felt or moleskin, which will also wear out but is easy and inexpensive to replace.

The bottom line for carbon arrow shooters is to find an arrow rest that is ruggedly and simply built yet offers the microadjustability necessary to achieve fletch clearance with these small-diameter shafts. More and more manufacturers offer arrow rests of this type each year.

CONCLUSION

How much can you expect to spend on a quality arrow rest for bowhunting? A quick look through several mail-order catalogs and discussions with both rest makers and pro shop owners reveals that you should be able to find what you want for $25 to $60. A top-of-the-line rest for the serious target shooter can cost three times that. Anything below that price range will probably be of inferior quality.

While manufacturers continue working to improve existing arrow rest designs, they'll tell you flat out not to expect any new "radical" designs in the near future. But that's all right. So many outstanding arrow rests are available at reasonable prices that it's already hard to sift through them all.

Robin Hood would be green with envy.

A big challenge for carbon shaft shooters: finding arrow rests that allow proper fletching clearance.

Accessories for Your Compound Bow

SIGHTING SYSTEMS

More than 90 percent of all bowhunters today use some sort of bow sight to help place their arrows where they want them. That's because the modern compound bow lends itself to being drawn and held for a reasonable length of time, which facilitates using a precision aiming device. And while "instinctive" shooters using no sighting system can and do take their share of game each fall, when it comes to placing your shaft with surgical precision shot after shot, there's no question that using some sort of bow sight is the way to go.

In addition to a bow sight, your bow's sighting system may also include accessory items like a peep sight (see page 35) and kisser button (see page 42). Some bowhunters, where it's legal, also use a small light for illuminating the top sight pin in dim light conditions.

TYPES OF BOW SIGHTS

There are four basic bow sight types: fixed-pin, moveable-pin, crosshair and pendulum. Each has advantages and disadvantages. Experimentation will help you find the one that's best for your own bowhunting.

Fixed-Pin Sights

Manufacturers sell more fixed-pin bow sights today than all other types combined. That's because they provide the unparalleled flexibility of several different sight pins that you can set for a precise distance. When you have a target at 20 yards, simply put the 20-yard pin on the spot you wish to hit, then draw and shoot. If the shot is 30 yards, move to the 30-yard pin and let your arrow fly. Shots taken when the target is not exactly at a distance for which you have a specific sight pin—as most shots at animals are—are sighted "between the pins." Easily switching between pins set at different distances is also a big advantage when game is moving, allowing the hunter to track the animal and change pins instantaneously. Also, you can add or remove sight pins as your needs dictate. For example, many treestand bowhunters set their sights up with just a single pin set between 15 and 25 yards, depending on the circumstances. They know that if an animal is a bit closer or farther than that distance, they can hold a little low or high and still make the shot. And because of the

Plain and simple fixed pins have worked well for decades and will continue to.

simple design of most fixed-pin sights, they can be built with few moving parts that can rattle loose under rigorous field conditions.

The choices of sight pin sizes and materials vary. Small-diameter pins work best with long distances and good light; larger-diameter pins are better in lower light. For many years the only pins available were either $^6/_{32}$ inches or $^8/_{32}$ inches in diameter, but now some sights, like the Sonoran Hunter, feature thin, .026-inch wire pins. Most metal sight pins are made from either brass or steel. However, fiber-optic sight pins are popular today, and most sight companies offer at least a few fiber-optic models in their bow sight lines. Not legal in all states, various lighted sight pins offer excellent low-light visibility. Cobra Manufacturing Co. offers lighted sight pins as well as the Light All sight light, which screws into the top of the pin guard and shines a light down on the sight pins.

Pendulum Sights

Designed specifically for the treestand bowhunter, pendulum sights feature a single horizontal crosswire or pin, which pivots on a hinge to rise as you take aim closer to the base of your tree and drops as you aim farther away. Combined with a fixed vertical stadia wire, the two give a precise aiming point out to 30 yards or so, the

exact distance being directly proportional to arrow speed and the height of the treestand. This eliminates the need for treestand hunters to aim high or low to compensate for the varying distance of their quarry from the stand, as well as the tendency of the bow to "shoot high" when using a standard pin-type sight from a high treestand.

Top-quality pendulum bow sights allow adjustment of the length of the pivoting arm, thereby fine-tuning the sight for your individual bow's arrow speed. Though many current pendulum sights do not have this feature, they can still yield acceptable accuracy once you dial them in. One disadvantage of pendulum sights is that some tend to be a bit noisy, and their moving parts tend to be somewhat fragile or can stick. All things considered, pendulum sights are an excellent tool for treestand bowhunting. There are several good pendulum sights on today's market, including those by made Keller, Saunders and Advanced Archery Products.

Pendulum sights take the guesswork out of shooting from a treestand.

Movable-Pin Sights

Hunters who favor a movable-pin bow sight do so for a couple of reasons. First, they like the fact that they have only one sight pin, which keeps them from getting confused and placing the wrong pin of a multiple-pin sight on the target during the heat of battle or having to shoot

The main benefit of a single, movable-pin sight: being able to adjust the pin to the accurate distance.

between the pins. Second, because the archer can adjust the movable pin and set it at a precise distance, he can guess the range to the target (or use a modern bowhunting range finder, which almost all proponents of movable-pin sights carry at all times), then quickly set the sight pin for that distance.

Movable-pin sights have a small but ardent following. Many Western bowhunters, faced with shots ranging from point-blank to 50 yards or more, love them. I also know several treestand whitetail hunters who like these sights too. These hunters set their lone sight pin for a different specific distance every time they change treestand locations.

Of course, there are trade-offs. When an animal is moving and the distance changes rapidly or when the animal appears suddenly out of the brush and the archer does not know the distance, the bowhunter must then guess the distance and would probably be better served with a multiple-pin sight. I've personally used a Sight Master movable-pin sight a fair amount and have found that it works very well. Martin Archery also makes quality sights of this type.

Crosshair Sights

Crosshair sights, also excellent bowhunting sights, feature horizontal and vertical stadia wires that give you both a distance and left-or-right

orientation. Early crosshair sights, favored by many bowhunters making the transition from rifle hunting, gave these novice archers a sight picture identical to the one they were used to with a rifle scope.

Many early versions of crosshair sights were cheaply made and easily broken, but hunters liked them because the sight picture was similar to the rifle scopes they were used to. One early crosshair sight I tested had plastic stadia wires that bent like wet spaghetti noodles. Today's top crosshair sight manufacturers—like Fine-Line, Cobra, Montana Sights, Hoyt USA, Game Tracker and PSE—build strong sights that can take just about anything the hard-charging bowhunter can dish out.

Crosshair sights offer both vertical and horizontal alignment.

WHAT TO LOOK FOR IN A BOWHUNTING SIGHT

Simply stated, the best bowhunting sights are built by manufacturers who know that serious bowhunters will beat up on their sights. And while providing important features, they build sights simply and with a minimum of screws and adjustment knobs that can shake loose during a season of hard hunting. Top-of-the-line bowhunting sights are also compact and lightweight.

The best sights must have independent vertical

and horizontal adjustments. However, many of today's sights also allow you to move the entire sight pin block as a single entity while maintaining the integrity of the sight. This is a great feature, especially if you sight the bow in, then bump the sight bracket or find the bow goes out of tune just a bit and you are forced to adjust the arrow rest or move the nock point slightly to regain the tune you want. You then must re-sight

on only one pin—usually a midrange pin—and the others will be either very close or exactly on the money. This will save you a bundle of time.

Never underestimate the importance of a rugged pin or stadia wire guard. A pin guard cannot be too beefy. In addition to the pin guard protecting the sight pins during shooting, you'll inevitably end up laying the bow down on the pin guard to avoid laying it on the bow's other

Peep Sights Are Definite Accuracy Enhancers

Almost all compound bow shooters use some type of peep sight as part of their total sighting system. A peep forces you to anchor consistently and keep your head erect, presenting the same sight picture shot after shot.

While some target shooters use peep sights with pinhole apertures, bowhunters need as large a peep hole as possible. You want to let in the maximum amount of light, which is critical when you're trying to find your pins or stadia wire at dawn or dusk. This large hole won't noticeably affect hunting accuracy. In the days before manufacturers began building peeps with oversized apertures, I used to drill out the aperture hole of my Fine-Line Zero Peep Sight with a quarter-inch drill. Today, peep sight manufacturers offer both oversized and adjustable apertures, making it easy for you to find the right size for your shooting. Both Game Tracker and Fine-Line also make peep sights using four small neon polycarbonate fibers that gather light, à la fiber-optic bow sight pins, which work well to help illuminate the viewing window in low-light conditions.

The disadvantage of peep sights is that

they block too much of the available light right at the cusp of dawn and dark, making it impossible to see your sight pins through the peep when light is so low. However, I find that by using a

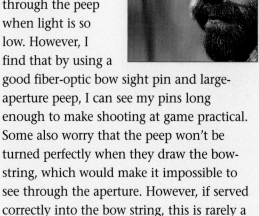

good fiber-optic bow sight pin and large-aperture peep, I can see my pins long enough to make shooting at game practical. Some also worry that the peep won't be turned perfectly when they draw the bowstring, which would make it impossible to see through the aperture. However, if served correctly into the bow string, this is rarely a problem, and many peep models use a piece of rubber tubing that pulls the peep into alignment for each and every shot.

I shoot so much more consistently when using a peep that I'm willing to sacrifice a few minutes of early and late shooting and take a bit of time every day to ensure my peep turns correctly. I bet you will too.

Choosing a Sight

With such a huge number of different bowhunting sight makes, models and designs on today's market, it's easy to find one that fits your shooting and hunting style. With sight design and technology changing rapidly, a well-stocked archery pro shop offers the best way to see what's out there. Look over several different makes, models and designs and ask the shop owner to let you shoot a couple of different sights on the indoor range to get a feel for them.

Buy the best bow sight you can afford. You should be able to find a top-notch hunting bow sight for $30 to $70. I have friends who have two different types of bow sights, exchanging them when they change their basic hunting technique. One serious bowhunter buddy of mine loves a pendulum sight for treestand deer and black bear hunting. But when he heads West to hunt mule deer and elk, he removes this sight and replaces it with a movable-pin sight. Like all parts of the hunting bow, it's an individual preference.

This is the only question you have to ask yourself: Does my sight help me shoot better?

side, where the bow quiver holds the arrow shafts, which might bend or be otherwise damaged. My favorite type of pin guard is a beefy, clear plastic model that does two things: protects the sight pins and allows additional light in for easier aiming in low-light situations.

It is also critical that the bow sight be attached securely to the bow's riser. On some bows, you mount the sight directly with two large screws, while for others you use a two-part dovetail mounting system. Here, you secure the mounting bracket to the riser with two large screws, with the sight itself able to slip in and out of the mounting bracket quickly and easily. The sight is usually held in place with a single, large screw with an oversized knob, which does two things: makes it quick and easy to detach the sight for transportation and allows you simply to reattach the sight in exactly the same place time and time again.

Here's a helpful hint: Use white paint or

Use a tough pin guard to make sure your pins don't get bent or bumped out of alignment.

an indelible marker and mark the edge of both the male dovetail and female dovetail bracket with the sight attached. This way you'll be sure that you're placing the sight in precisely the same position every time, assuring a consistent point of impact. To minimize any noise that may be created during the shot at the point where the bow sight attaches to the riser, I pad both the riser and the bottom of my sight's dovetail bracket with a small piece of stick-on felt before bolting the bracket down.

Fiber-Optic Sight Pins

Fiber-optic sight pins use semitransparent colored plastic pins that gather a large amount of the available natural light, which ends up in the sight pin tip, appearing to glow lightly in dim light. The bowhunter can now see the sight pins better during the most critical portions of the day—dawn and dusk—than he or she ever could when using old-style steel or brass pins.

Fiber-optic pins come in three basic colors: lime green, yellow and red. For me, lime green pins show up best in dim light, while red pins are the easiest to see during normal daylight conditions. Because I personally won't take shots longer than 30 yards during the dimmest light of legal-shooting hours, on my own bow sights the top two pins are lime green and set for 20 and 30 yards, followed by a pair of red pins set for 40 and 50 yards. Your eyes may see the other sight pin colors differently in varying light conditions, so before buying a fiber-optic sight, don't forget to test this at your local archery pro shop.

The plastic construction of fiber-optic sight pins makes them more fragile than metal pins. To that end, make sure the sights you are considering have a sight pin guard that is large and sturdy enough to protect the pins from accidental bumps and bruises that could snap them in the field. It is also important that the sight design allow lots of natural light to hit the pins themselves. Sights with small pin guards or smallish sight pins will not glow as brightly in the dimmest light as those with larger pin guards and lengthier sight pins. To keep the fiber-optic pins compact, yet provide enough pin length to maximize light gathering, many companies have bent their pins into a U-shaped design, which works very well.

While ideally suited for treestand bowhunting, ruggedly built fiber-optic bow sights are also a good choice for almost all spot-and-stalk hunting situations. I use them for virtually all my bowhunting today, from Western backpack hunts to treestand whitetail hunting.

Fiber-optic sight technology is still in its infancy, so you can expect to see rapid advances over the next few years in both the pins themselves and the design of the sights. Currently, all models of hunting bow sights offer fiber optics. Unlike lighted sight pins, fiber optics are legal in all 50 states, and the Pope and Young Club accepts qualifying animals taken while hunting with fiber optics for record-book entry.

QUIVERS

*I*n the days of yore, archers toted their arrow shafts in some sort of quiver slung over their shoulders. Much later came quivers carried on the hip. Finally, archers found that the most convenient way to transport their arrow shafts was in a quiver that attached directly to the bow itself.

The Archery Manufacturer's and Merchant's Association (AMO) defines quiver quite simply: "A device for holding a quantity of arrows. Can be attached to the bow or be of the design to be worn by the archer." Regardless of design type, all except the most old-style back quivers feature a hood, which holds and protects your broadheads, and a series of arrow shaft grippers, which holds the lower end of the shafts. Quivers must also hold your arrows in the ready-to-use position, where you can quickly and easily remove them for shooting.

A basic question you must answer is whether you want to use a bow-attached or non-bow-attached quiver for bowhunting.

WHAT TYPE OF QUIVER IS BEST?

The answer to what type of quiver will work for you rests on you discovering what's most important to you as a bowhunter. In the small debate about which type of quiver is best for bowhunting, some claim that using a bow-attached quiver causes excessive bow torque, an overbearing weight imbalance, poor accuracy and potentially missed shots at game. Others, many of whom are serious bowhunters or bow-attached quiver makers, don't buy that argument.

WHO'S RIGHT?

Here's what Randy Ulmer, one of the best all-time 3-D tournament shooters and a highly accomplished bowhunter, has to say: "Does a bow-attached quiver affect accuracy? The answer would have to be yes. But does it make any real difference in terms of accuracy in bowhunting? No, it does not."

"Tournament shooters will not use a bow quiver because it will affect accuracy to a very small degree, and in a game where fractions of an inch can mean the difference between winning and losing, you can't afford this," Ulmer explains. "But, to me, the convenience of a bow-attached quiver when hunting overrides any small accuracy problems it might cause. I've not yet missed a shot at an animal because of my bow quiver."

Just how much can a bow-attached quiver affect hunting bow accuracy, especially when you start emptying the quiver by shooting more than one arrow? President of Sagittarius (the country's leading maker of bow quivers) serious and accomplished bowhunter Jim Velasquez has done some testing on this subject and believes a bow quiver's effects on hunting accuracy are minimal.

"Years ago we made a shooting machine because we wanted to see what the differences would be with and without a bow quiver and without human error affecting the shooting," Velasquez describes. "We shot more than 400 arrows out to 40 yards, using four, six and eight arrows in the quiver. We saw a very insignificant difference in point of impact in comparison to a bow shot with no quiver attached. When we went down from eight arrows to one arrow in the quiver, we did see a small but very insignificant point of impact change, but it wasn't enough to make any difference in a person's ability to hit a kill zone in hunting situations."

BOW-ATTACHED QUIVERS

The vast majority of bowhunters today—ever since the late 1950s and early 1960s— use some sort of bow-attached quiver. Bowhunters simply prefer its convenience over other quiver types. With a bow quiver, your arrows are always with your bow and they're always easy to grab. All quiver manufacturers emphasize that if you hunt with a bow-attached quiver, it is important to tune your bow with the quiver attached and also to practice shooting that way too. Tuning a bow without the quiver, then randomly attaching one the day before hunting season begins, would guarantee inaccurate shooting.

One-piece and two-piece bow quivers are avail-

able. A one-piece bow quiver has a hood that is riveted or screwed tightly to the mounting bracket and that is large enough to cover the broadheads completely to protect you from being accidentally cut. Also, the quiver must have rubber arrow shaft grippers attached firmly to the mounting bracket that will firmly grip the shafts, keeping them from slipping or vibrating. The grippers should fit the type of shaft specifically; aluminum and carbon shafts require different sizes.

Two-piece bow quivers have separate hood and shaft-gripper pieces. Most attach to the bow using bolts inserted through special holes drilled through the riser itself, but a few use brackets that slip under the limb bolts. Favored by those who never remove their quivers when hunting, two-piece quivers are both lighter and quieter than one-piece models.

Treestand hunters often use quick-detach bow quivers, which offer them the best of both worlds: the convenience of transporting arrows attached to the bow into the field, where they can then quickly detach the quiver from the bow and hang

Bow-attached quiver.

it in the tree next to their treestand. But quick-detach quivers do not work well for shooting at game when attached to the bow; their construction makes them too noisy.

BACK QUIVERS

Little more than a tube made from cured leather into which arrow shafts were randomly dropped, the first primitive back quiver was carried with a leather strap slung across the shoulders. The disadvantages to these quivers are obvious: they allowed arrows to bang against each other, often damaging the shaft and dulling broadhead blades. Also, shafts could fall out easily, a dangerous happenstance.

Modern back quivers, such as the Cat Quiver, are adjustable, have protection for both broadheads and fletching and hold shafts tightly in place to prevent noise and damage. A well-built product, the Cat Quiver features a pair of backpack-like shoulder straps and a small daypack on top.

Hip quiver.

HIP QUIVERS

Hip quivers are worn on the belt, with the arrow fletchings facing forward. Target archers were the first to use hip quivers, and top-quality hip quivers for these shooters feature a place to hold a small notebook, mini-binoculars and other small items. Until the mid-1980s, hip quivers did not find favor with bowhunters. But in the mid-1980s many bowhunters, in an attempt to achieve the ultimate in accuracy by removing bow-attached quivers, started using them again.

Some hip quivers feature a leather string tie to secure the lower portion around the leg and keep the quiver from bouncing around while you're hiking. Some hunters also pad the outer surfaces with fleece or felt to quiet the quiver against brush. The best have solid broadhead hoods and high-quality rubber arrow shaft grippers.

I've tried hip quivers and personally don't like them. Out West they seem to bang and bump against brush too much and cause problems when I'm trying to crawl on game. I have used a hip quiver satisfactorily when treestand hunting, where I can hang it next to me in the tree. But it's a personal thing. I know a handful of bowhunters who like hip quivers and wouldn't ever use a bow quiver again. To each his own.

Back quiver.

OTHER ACCESSORIES

*I*n addition to the basics of bow accessories discussed earlier—arrow rest, bow sight and quiver—there are several other accessory items you may or may not choose to add to your bow, and a myriad of other small accessory items that will make shooting easier and more pleasant. Accessory items not listed here, like bow tuning tools, will be discussed in later chapters.

Arm Guard

Though it does not attach to your bow, an arm guard is an essential accessory. Though its primary purpose is to prevent a painful "slap" on the forearm from the bowstring, as a bowhunter, I find my arm guard more important as a means to hold my shirt and coat sleeves in tight to my forearm, where they cannot inadvertently catch the bowstring and ruin a shot. Made from plastic or leather, with the best for bowhunting covered with a quiet fleece, arm guards attach to the arm with stretch bands held in place with Velcro.

Bow Case

You need a soft bow case padded with foam for general use and a hard case made from aluminum or hard plastic if you fly to your hunting destination. Soft cases should have an oversized zipper and separate exterior pockets for arrow shafts and smaller items. Hard cases can carry one or two bows plus accessories. They should have strong latches and hinges, and be able to be locked securely.

Bow Sling

A bow sling can make packing your bow around the woods much easier. There are several different types of slings, including those that attach permanently to the bow and others that slip over the limbs and can be easily removed so they don't interfere with your shooting.

Broadhead Wrench

You should never attach or remove broadheads from your shafts without using a broadhead wrench. A wrench will protect you from those razor-sharp blades that have a nasty habit of slicing unprotected fingers. Most broadheads come packaged with a wrench.

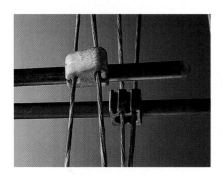

Cable Guard

All compound bows have a cable guard bar, which keeps the arrow fletching off the cables at the shot. A cable slide is used to prevent excess cable wear and noise. Most bows come with cheap plastic cable slides that can squeak and groan, especially when they're wet or cold. Definitely worth considering, aftermarket cable slides cost only a few bucks, feature rollers that slide effortlessly over the cable bar and are very quiet.

Kisser Button

A kisser button—a small plastic disk that attaches to the bowstring—serves the same essen-

tial function as a peep sight: to ensure a consistent anchor point. At full draw, the kisser button touches the corner of your mouth on the lips (hence the name) and helps you keep your head position consistent, thus ensuring a consistent sight picture. While most bowhunters use a peep sight, some prefer the kisser button.

Moleskin

Stick-on moleskin is one of the handiest items you can carry. Bowhunters routinely cut it into perfectly-sized pieces and place it on the bow shelf and sight window to prevent game-spooking noise should an arrow be accidentally dropped. I also use it to pad the areas between parts bolted onto my bow, including the arrow rest, bow sight, quiver and stabilizer. You can also use moleskin as a silencer on arrow rest prongs and arms.

Nocks

Nock sets, used to establish the nocking point on the bowstring, clamp onto the string with a pair of pliers. The best are made from brass and have a rubber insert to protect the string. You should always carry extra nock sets in your tackle box. (See more in this section on tackle boxes.)

Silencer

A string silencer will dissipate excess string vibration at the shot, reducing bow noise. Silencers are made from rubber (commonly called cat whiskers), fleece or yarn. If you use string silencers, you need a pair of them, one each above and below the nocking point.

Stabilizer

A stabilizer performs three tasks: it adds some weight to the bow, helps balance the bow in the shooter's hand and absorbs vibration and noise. A hunting stabilizer is relatively short—under 8 inches in length, and often half that—while a target stabilizer can be more than 2 feet long. Some bowhunters swear by them, but others don't like their added weight and size. However, most people do shoot their bows better with a stabilizer attached. Stabilizers are needed mostly on two-cam bows with radical speed cams. The new hydraulic models provide excellent performance in a compact package and are worth checking out.

Tackle Box

A small tackle box is the best way in the world to store and transport all the little things you'll accumulate as a bowhunter: spare parts, lubricating devices, tuning tools, booklets and more. MTM Products makes a great box designed expressly for bowhunters.

Bowstring Wax

Modern synthetic bowstrings don't require the lubrication that old-style strings did. However, periodically waxing your string with string wax will both lubricate it and help protect it from minor nicks obtained in the field. Both natural beeswax and synthetic waxes work well.

Wrist Slings

Wrist slings prevent you from dropping the bow at the shot with a relaxed hand—recommended form for good shooting. A sling—a loop made from leather or nylon—attaches to the bow below the grip, looping over the wrist. Some bowhunters love them; others hate them. They're worth looking into.

Chapter 3

FINGERS VS. RELEASE AIDS

*H*ow you release the bowstring—either with your fingers or by using a mechanical release aid—says a lot about you.

These days, fingers shooters tend to be conservative traditionalists. Even if they choose a modern compound bow over a recurve or longbow, they believe that simple is better, that there's no need for one more piece of machinery that just might malfunction at the wrong time. And while they understand the need for technology in today's world, it tends to scare them a bit too.

Release shooters are pragmatists. "Let's cut to the chase," they might say. "If a release will make me a better shooter, why bother with fingers?" They want to be the best shooters they can be, and realize—pragmatically—that in today's on-the-go world, they just don't have the time to devote to learning to shoot consistently with their fingers.

It is much a function of today's fast-paced world—where 30-second sound bites and *USA Today*–sized news stories shape our thinking on everything from world peace and politics to how nature works—that the release aid has taken over archery. Industry insiders estimate that 80 to 90 percent of all bowhunters use a release aid today, a complete reversal of those same statistics just a decade ago. Learning to shoot a bow accurately, then recapturing that accuracy after a lengthy lay-off, can be done much more quickly and efficiently with a release than with fingers. That fact is a huge reason why releases dominate the market.

Yet something about the simplicity of fingers still greatly appeals to me. While I now shoot a release most of the time, I still get my fingers bow out every now and then. I feel a stronger connection to the long history and tradition of bowhunting when shooting fingers, something that puzzles me somewhat. It takes a while, but soon I can lay them in there with my fingers just like I used to, and that makes me feel good inside.

Fingers or release aid? There's more to the decision than simply how well you can shoot on the target range or in the deer woods. To a large degree, it's a lot about who you are and where you're going as a bowhunter. And best of all, there's no right or wrong choice to be made, only the choice that pleases you the most.

THE SIMPLICITY OF FINGERS

As the sport of bowhunting has progressed over the past several decades, the available equipment has become increasingly diverse and complex. From simple longbows and recurves to the cables and wheels of the modern compound bow and its seemingly endless array of options and accessories, from the simple cedar arrow shaft to the aluminum, carbon and aluminum-carbon composite shafts of today, choosing the right bow-and-arrow setup can be downright intimidating.

The way the arrow shaft is released from the string has also evolved. From the simple use of one's own fingers, a new world of mechanical devices designed to do that job for you becomes increasingly popular. Further complicating the bow shooting equation, "release aids," as these devices are more commonly known, come in

several basic designs, shapes and sizes.

Today, far more archers release their arrows using a mechanical release aid than their fingers. Be that as it may, a small cadre of bowhunters believe that they increase their chances of success in the field by using a tried-and-true fingers release.

When I started bowhunting seriously in college in the early 1970s, shooting with one's fingers was the only viable option available—compound bows had only just been invented and we didn't really know much about them. A calf's hair tab or all-leather shooting glove was the only assist we used in releasing our shafts from our old Bear Archery Kodiak take-down recurves.

FINGER CONCERNS

Using your fingers is simple, which is the primary advantage it has over the use of a release aid while bowhunting. Proponents of fingers believe that Murphy lurks everywhere, just waiting to throw a monkey wrench into the works to screw up their chances. Their motto is "simple and reliable is best" when it comes to all their bowhunting equipment. After all, if you break your fingers while hunting, you have a lot more to worry about than whether or not you can release an arrow shaft. You're probably not going to lose or misplace your fingers, either—they're always going to be there, making them quicker to use than a mechanical release aid. Also, your fingers hug the arrow nock during draw, helping guard against the possibility of accidental disengagement.

The potential lack of dependability is what worries most fingers shooters about switching to a mechanical release aid. Ten years ago, this would have been a legitimate concern. But today, hunting release aids are extremely reliable and will perform under the most trying conditions. On the other hand, with a release aid there is always the possibility of pre-releasing an arrow. Release aids can also cause excessive wear on bowstrings, and they are inherently more noisy than shooting with fingers.

THE MECHANICS OF A FINGER RELEASE

Most fingers shooters—but certainly not all—use some sort of tab or glove to protect their fingers from the abrasive bowstring. When placing the string hand on the bowstring itself, most shooters place the index finger above the nock point, and the middle and ring fingers below the arrow nock, touching the string at the first joint. The hand is naturally inclined and the bow drawn with shoulder muscles, not the muscles of the hand and fingers. Most of the bowstring's weight is felt on the middle finger, with the other two fingers applying minimal tension.

Fingers shooters generally anchor the bow in one of two places. Most bowhunters—including me—anchor by placing the index finger at the corner of the mouth. Target shooters seem to prefer placing the index finger under the corner of the jaw. Regardless of which you choose, make sure you anchor in exactly the same place every time.

When you've achieved the sight picture you want and it's time to loose the arrow, the key is to relax the fingers, not jerk them open. The bowstring should slide easily and naturally off your fingers. I try to concentrate on keeping my elbow high and pulling with my back, at the same time relaxing my fingers so that the string simply goes as if I had nothing to do with it. Many fingers shooters make the error of "plucking" the string. You'll know you've released the shaft properly if your hand slides smoothly and effortlessly back along your face, your fingers nice and relaxed.

All things being equal, for most shooters, using a mechanical release aid will help them shoot their bows more accurately than when using fingers. That's why in tournament competition, each style of shooting is separated into different categories; fingers shooters don't have a chance against the precision of release-aid users.

That's on the target range. In practical terms, a skilled fingers shooter can more than hold his own when bowhunting. Many more variables are involved when it comes to harvesting game—distance judgment, stalking skill, stand placement, playing the wind, uphill and downhill angles and the speed at which you have to release the shaft, to name a few—that will determine whether or not you eat venison or store-bought beef this year. For many bowhunters, that means keeping it simple and using their fingers.

Use a consistent anchor point, then relax your fingers (don't jerk them). These factors are essential to finger-release accuracy.

*U*sing a finger tab or shooting glove not only prevents wear and tear on your skin but also provides the ultimate in a smooth fingers release.

GLOVES

Shooting gloves were the first protective device worn by archers. While some traditional bowhunters still use them, most have gone to a shooting tab instead. Still, shooting gloves will get the job done.

Shooting glove.

Just like a regular glove, a shooting glove has individual finger stalls. Most gloves are made from a supple leather, which doesn't give your fingers a whole lot of protection from an abrasive bowstring. Grooves can also form in the stalls over time, which can catch the string at the time of release, hampering smoothness. Also, because your fingers like to "do their own thing," there is more potential for a jerky release than when using a tab.

FINGER TABS

For bowhunting, a better choice is a finger tab, which is simply a solid section of leather or plastic used to protect the fingers. A small ring of either plastic, leather or rubber fits over the middle fingers of the shooting hand, holding the tab in place.

A finger tab offers a number of advantages.

First, the solid face of the tab prevents your fingers from working out of sync with each other, promoting a more consistent release than a shooting glove does. Second, you can rotate tabs away from your palm and wear them over the back of your hand—keeping them out of the way when hiking or performing other dexterous functions—then quickly rotating them into place when a shot opportunity arises. Third, in cold weather you can slip a tab over a warm glove, shooting with no adjustments necessary. And lastly, tabs are inexpensive, making it easy to carry a spare or two at all times in case you misplace one.

The string face of shooting tabs is made from a number of materials. Old-style tabs have a face of calf's hair, which is slick and excellent until the hair starts to wear off. Some tabs have a smooth bare leather face, which is great. Others have a face of smooth plastic, which is the most durable of all and is impervious to moisture. I like the calf's hair tabs, but that's a personal choice.

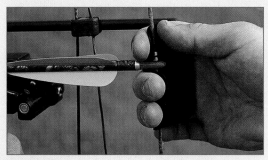

Finger tab.

A quality shooting tab has a finger spacer, which helps prevent the shooter from pinching the bowstring. Located on the back side of the tab, the spacer fits between the index and middle fingers. Without the spacer, it is possible to pinch the arrow nock hard enough that it will add undue bending to the arrow at the time of release, causing erratic arrow flight.

The Precision of Release Aids

In August 1993, I was bowhunting Dall sheep in Alaska when I had a small accident. The horse's saddle cinch broke, and my saddle rolled to the side. Trying to keep myself upright, I shoved the saddle horn, hoping to roll the saddle back upright and keep from tumbling onto the rocks. It worked, but in the process I cracked a bone in the back of my right hand. Every time I exerted pressure on that hand—like drawing my bow with my fingers—it brought tears to my eyes.

I was out of business as a bowhunter. I was leaving for an elk hunt in two weeks and was sick. What was I going to do? In desperation, I tried using a wrist-strap-type mechanical release aid. The strap took all the pressure of drawing the bow off my wrist, placing it instead on my back muscles. And it didn't hurt! I taped up my hand, retuned my bow and was back in business. As I continued to practice with my release aid, I was amazed at how well I began shooting. My arrow groups tightened right up, and those disgusting "flyers" all but disappeared. Soon I was putting five broadhead-tipped arrows into a 6-inch square from the 50-yard line. I had to quit shooting more than one broadhead at the same spot, as I was continually cutting the fletching off the shafts. The big 6x6 bull I took three weeks later would never have been mine had I not switched to a release.

Release Aid Benefits

Precision is the big advantage of mechanical release-aids. As mentioned earlier, in target tournaments, release-aid shooters have their own class, simply because no fingers shooter can come close to matching the precision with which arrows can be shot with a mechanical release aid. Release aids do, without question, make you the best bow shot you can be.

Another closely related benefit of using a release aid is consistency. With fingers, you grip the bowstring across a wide area, usually two or three fingers covered by a shooting glove or tab. All that contact surface makes it extremely difficult to release the string exactly the same every time. On the other hand, a release aid grips the string at only one or two small contact points, enabling the string to slide free the same way shot after shot.

With a release aid, tired shooters can still perform up to their potential. Say that after hiking hard all day long, you are bone-tired. All of a sudden, a mule deer, elk, black bear—or whatever your quarry is—suddenly appears, and you're in position for a shot. Your fatigued arms, hands and fingers may let you down, effecting a release that's not quite the same as your normal release, potentially causing a poor shot. But with a release aid, your fatigue won't be much of a factor at all. If you can draw and hold the bow steady, you just have to squeeze the trigger, and the arrow flies as it normally does.

Extreme cold can produce the same effect. When your hands are so cold you can barely move them, shooting with fingers becomes a real chore. Wearing a shooting tab over a thick glove just doesn't feel the same as it does when you're wearing a thinner, warm-weather glove. With a release aid, it's not a problem. Again, simply squeeze the trigger and perfect arrow flight is assured.

That's not to say that switching from fingers to a release aid will transform you into Robin Hood overnight. It won't. It takes practice, a well-tuned bow, more practice, an ability to judge distance, more practice, skill at uphill and downhill angle shots, and even more practice to get where you want to be.

RELEASE AID CONCERNS

There are three major concerns when shooting with a release aid.

Anchor Point

The first concern is a consistent anchor point. When shooting with fingers, placing the index finger of the shooting hand in the corner of your mouth or using a kisser button are easy ways to ensure a consistent anchor point. With most release aids, this doesn't work. You have to develop your own consistent method of returning to the same anchor point time after time. When using my wrist-strap release, I place the knuckle of my thumb at the back of my jawbone.

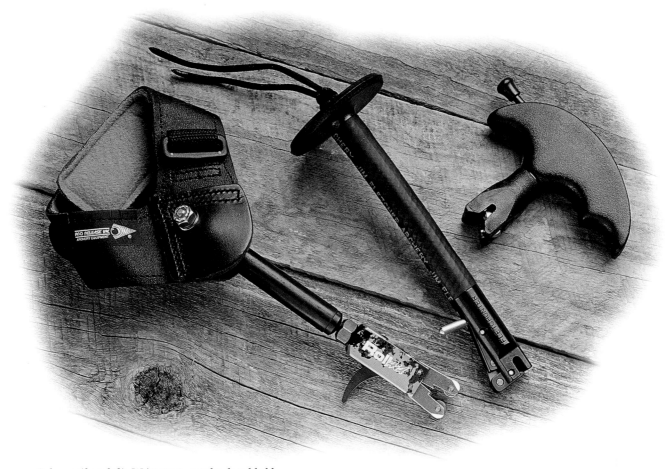

Releases (from left): Wrist strap, concho, hand-held.

The String Loop

A string loop, sometimes called a "release rope," is nothing more than a small loop of heavy-duty nylon string or rope permanently attached to the bowstring. Basically, instead of using a standard nock set, you tie the loop above and below the arrow nock, leaving just enough room once the arrow has been nocked to clip on the jaws of the release aid. In a nutshell, the string loop acts as both the nock set and the connector between the release aid and bowstring.

One of the first people to promote the use of a string loop for bowhunters was Pete Shepley, president of PSE, a highly accomplished bowhunter who uses one himself.

"The string loop relieves the unbalanced pressures on the arrow nock/string contact point," Shepley told me during a break in a Texas deer hunt a few years ago. "It makes the shot quieter, prevents unnecessary bowstring serving wear, and if you use a release aid that does not attach itself to your wrist with a strap, you can attach the release aid to the string loop and leave it there while sitting in your treestand."

THE DOWNSIDE

String loops do have some disadvantages. First, tying them can be a son of a gun and will frustrate even the most patient person until he or she finally figures it out. Second, they can be a bit slow to use in the field, though I've never had a loop cause me to miss a shot opportunity. Third, arrow nocks must fit the bowstring snugly to prevent them from falling off the string when drawing the bow. And fourth, the string loop works best with caliper release aids, being much less effective with ball-bearing releases.

But I find that the advantages of the string loop far outweigh the disadvantages. Using a string loop seems to make bow tuning much easier and quicker. I've used a loop on hunts ranging from minus 50°F to 100°F and have never had a problem shooting an accurate arrow.

As Shepley told me in Texas, "Once you start shooting a string loop, you'll never go back to shooting without one." So far, in my case at least, he's right.

Adding a peep sight will also ensure a consistent anchor point. Many release shooters touch the bowstring with the tip of their nose at full draw, giving them three reference points for their anchor: thumb knuckle at the back of the jaw, nose on the bowstring and looking through the peep sight with the head erect. This formula makes for very consistent shooting.

Premature Release

The second major concern with release aids is a premature release. This can occur during the draw if you let your finger get near the trigger. To prevent this, on my trigger-style release I make sure to put my trigger finger behind the trigger as I come to full draw, moving it into position only when I've found my anchor point.

Releases from left: rope loop (left) and metal jaws. Jaws are better in almost all hunting situations.

Reliability

Reliability is the third concern. In the beginning, cheaply made release aids were easy to find; malfunctions were not unheard of. Also, snow, ice and mud jammed some release aid mechanisms to the point that they reacted sluggishly, if at all, when the shooter touched the trigger. But today, the best release aids are precision tools designed to take the abuse a serious bowhunter will dish out. I've shot a bucketful of different release aid designs and styles over the past several years and have yet to find one from a reliable company that has let me down in this regard.

To help eliminate potential malfunctions in the field, try the following. In dry, dusty conditions, wash the release aid down with a good solvent to remove all oil and grease. Grease will pick up dirt, dust and grit that can lock up the mechanism. In wet weather, oil the release to keep it from rusting. In extreme cold, lubricate the release aid with

powdered graphite, which will not freeze like light machine oil will. Following this program, one season I used the same Scott Mongoose release problem-free in temperatures ranging from a humid 90°F during the early whitetail season in the South to *minus* 50°F degrees on a Northwest Territories muskox hunt.

RELEASE AID DESIGNS

There are three basic styles of release aids: wrist strap, concho and finger-held. Most bowhunters use a wrist-strap model of some sort. By keeping the wrist strap buckled around your wrist at all times, you're not only ready to go on a moment's notice, but you practically eliminate the chances of losing the release aid in the field. Smaller and lighter than wrist-strap releases, finger-held releases are growing in popularity. A small minority of bowhunters use concho releases.

Wrist Strap Release Aids

With wrist-strap release aids, all the pressure is on the back muscles when drawing the bow. This is an advantage because you can more easily draw your bow using your back than with your arms and hands; it also takes the pressure off your fingers, leaving them relaxed and loose when it's time to squeeze the trigger. With a concho (hand-held) release, you pull with your arms and fingers as well as your back.

Finger Release Aids

Some treestand hunters have begun switching from wrist-strap releases to smallish finger releases. With a finger release, you can set your bow in a stationary bow holder attached to the floor of the treestand, then clip the finger-held release directly to the bowstring and leave it there while waiting for a deer to come by. This leaves your hands free in the stand, and you also don't have to worry about clipping the release onto the bowstring in the excitement of the moment. All you have to do is lift the bow from the holder while grabbing the release at the same time, then draw and shoot. Again, this is a personal preference but something worth trying.

There are two main ways a release aid attaches

to the bowstring: with a rope or with metal jaws. While rope releases are easy on bowstrings and popular with target shooters, I think they're too slow to use in all but the most controlled hunting situations. Metal-jawed caliper or ball-bearing releases—the most popular on today's market—are simple to use, reliable and provide a smooth release.

The more you practice with a release, the quicker you'll be able to get it into action. While releases are slower than fingers, I've come to believe that, with practice, most bowhunters will never consider them too slow to use. I like to practice nocking an arrow and clamping my release aid onto the bow-string with my eyes closed so that it becomes second nature.

The bottom line with a release aid is that, all things being equal, using one will make you a better shot. Period. By being able to group your arrows more tightly, you'll extend your personal maximum shooting range a bit, assuming you can correctly estimate distances to the target. Better, more consistent shooting lends itself to confidence, without which success is not possible. And that's what all bowhunters try to achieve.

MAKING THE SWITCH

First off, there is no right or wrong way to shoot your bow. Whatever works best for you and whatever you're most comfortable with and confident in is the way to go. A decade ago, a survey of bowhunters nationwide showed that nearly 75 percent shot with their fingers and either a shooting tab or glove, while about 25 percent used a mechanical release aid. Today, the results are reversed and more. Industry surveys show that 80 to 90 percent of all bowhunters—especially newcomers to the sport—use some sort of release aid.

In shooting with a release aid, I've discovered that although I still have to practice regularly to remain a consistently good shot, after a lay-off I return to good shooting more quickly than I have when shooting with my fingers. That's due both to the consistency of the release when using the mechanical device as opposed to fingers, and to the fact that release-aid shooters primarily use

their back muscles at full draw, while fingers shooters must also use some hand and wrist muscles that quickly get out of shape.

If you plan to try switching from fingers to a release aid, or vice versa, remember that you must retune your bow. Arrows released with fingers oscillate from side to side at the time of release, while those shot with a release aid porpoise, or oscillate up and down. Remember: The appropriate arrow rest is also critical when shooting with either style. The tried-and-true cushion-plunger rest is the most popular with fingers shooters, while most release aid shooters use a shoot-through-type rest.

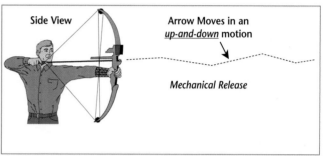

Side View — Arrow Moves in an *up-and-down* motion

Mechanical Release

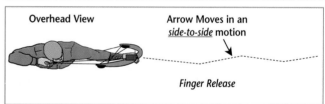

Overhead View — Arrow Moves in an *side-to-side* motion

Finger Release

Regardless of whether or not you use a release aid or shoot with fingers protected by a tab or glove, be sure to carry at least one spare into the field at all times just in case. I usually have a spare release aid or finger tab in either my daypack or the cargo pocket on my right pants leg plus have another spare back at camp. Better to be safe than sorry.

Smooth and quiet, modern release aids are as reliable as the sunrise. When shopping for a release, visit an archery pro shop and shoot several different makes and models on their indoor lanes. This way, you can compare apples to apples, and you'll come away with a release that feels good in your hand, fits your shooting and hunting style and produces maximum accuracy. Expect to spend $30 to $70 for a quality hunting release aid.

Chapter 4

ARROW SHAFTS

*T*here's something lethally romantic about a quiver full of hunting arrows. The sleek lines, colorful fletching and dangerous-looking arrowheads have an allure that draws bowhunters both to admire and respect them. It's been that way for thousands of years.

Selecting the proper arrow shaft is certainly one of the most important things a bowhunter will ever do. Is it more important than choosing the right bow? Than tuning your bow and sighting it in? Than picking the right tree to sit in? Absolutely.

With all the other pieces of equipment bowhunters need and the hunting strategies required to put them to use, it's easy to forget the one basic fact around which all bowhunting success is built: The object of the entire exercise is to place a razor-sharp broadhead precisely into the quarry's vitals. Your arrow shafts must be the right length and spine, perfectly straight, fletched properly and built with a quality arrow point insert and nock system, or your chances of placing that shaft consistently into the X-ring are zero.

Fortunately, modern bowhunters have the finest selection of arrow shafts and shaft-making components ever developed. From the romance and tradition of wooden shafts to the function and reliability of aluminum arrows to the space-age technology and high-tech performance of carbon and aluminum-carbon composite shafts, finding top-of-the-line arrow-making components is as easy as visiting your local archery pro shop or sifting through the pages of a specialty catalog. There is widespread, easy-to-understand information available for choosing shafts of the proper spine for your individual bow—and for building your own arrows, should you choose to do so.

Still, making the right choice involves a little education. With some knowledge about the history of arrow shafts, how arrows are made, why they're made that way, and where manufacturers believe we're headed in the coming years, you can make an informed decision. Understanding the performance characteristics of each shaft type will allow you to choose just the right one for your bowhunting needs.

Come explore the details of the arrow shaft. You won't think of it as "grabbing some arrows" ever again.

BASIC SHAFT COMPONENTS

Whom most people consider arrow shafts, they think first and foremost about the shaft itself. Is it wood, aluminum or carbon? How long is it? How heavy is it? What poundage and draw length bow will it shoot best from?

People don't often consider shaft components, those little parts that turn a bare arrow shaft into a missile. And that's a mistake. Without well-matched components—made to exact tolerances and precisely attached to the shaft—the arrow has no chance at all of flying straight and true.

ARROW NOCKS

Nocks are one of the most overlooked of all the components that make up a well-tuned bow-and-arrow system. Yet with the wrong nock—or the right nock attached poorly to the shaft—you're sure to experience disaster.

Located at the rear of the shaft, the nock is the portion of the shaft that snaps securely onto the bowstring. The nock should fit the string snugly yet should not be so tight that it unduly grabs the string at the shot.

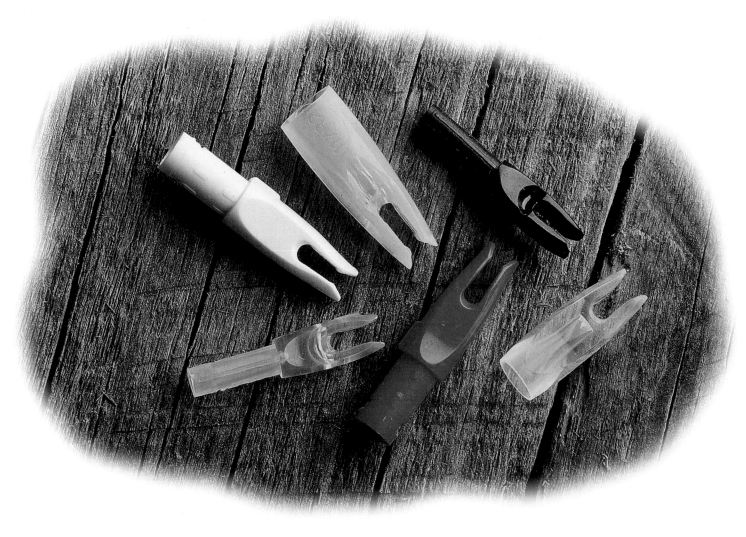

Many archers judge nock fit by snapping an arrow into the string, then turning the bow upside down so the shaft hangs from the string. The nock should hold the arrow in this position indefinitely but should release it when you gently "thump" the string with your index finger. Release-aid shooters—to prevent the arrow from falling off the string when they draw the bow—generally like their nocks to fit the string a bit tighter than fingers shooters do.

Consistency is critical with arrow nocks. All your arrows should have the same type and size nock, and they should all grip the string the same. Never mix and match arrow nocks.

Most critical is that the nock be fitted perfectly straight onto the arrow shaft. Crooked nocks tend to push the shaft to the side at the moment of release, destroying accuracy. Here's one way to check nock straightness: Hold the shaft loosely in one hand and blow gently on the arrow fletching, causing the shaft to spin. A crooked nock will appear to wobble as the shaft spins. If that happens, replace the nock immediately.

The introduction of the adjustable, or tunable, nock has been a big advance in recent years. For decades, archers affixed one-piece arrow nocks to the shaft by gluing them on. Although that does work well, once you've glued the nock in place it is in that position forever. Nock position, which controls the position of your fletching in relation to the arrow rest and bow riser, is critical in the bow tuning process. If your nock is permanently glued in place and your fletching is hitting the arrow rest, you'll have a heck of a time trying to tune that shaft perfectly.

A tunable nock is a two-piece product featuring the nock itself and either an insert or outsert that securely attaches to the shaft into which the nock fits. Now you can turn the nock, minutely adjust-

ing its position, which allows you to adjust the position of the fletching in relation to the arrow rest. Greatly simplifying the bow tuning process, this simple product also makes it easy to switch the same arrows between different bows. I will never again use nocks that are not easily tunable.

ARROW FLETCHING

In the old days, I used natural feathers to fletch all my arrow shafts. That was all that was available, and I figured that if it was good enough for Robin Hood, it was good enough for me.

But of course, there were problems.

In wet weather, natural feathers compress, losing their ability to steer the arrow shaft. Fragile, natural feathers also break or tear relatively easily. I quickly learned that it was vitally important to protect my feather fletching at all times.

Then along came plastic vanes. In my mind, a plastic vane's superior durability is its most important attribute. Quality vanes made from urethane, mylar or vinyl—and there are some cheap ones to

Adjustable nocks are fitted with bushings and allow you to turn the nock. This way you can adjust the nock until you have fletching clearance on your arrow rest.

What Size and Position of Arrow Fletching Is Best?

One of the purposes of fletching is to give the arrow shaft a rapid spin as it flies through the air—much like the rifling in a gun barrel spins a bullet—which stabilizes the shaft in flight.

Generally speaking, the larger the fletching, the better its ability to steer a broadhead-tipped arrow shaft on a straight path. Bowhunters who choose large-diameter broadheads should use larger fletching, while those using smaller-diameter heads can get by with slightly smaller fletching.

Fletching should also match the shaft size. Larger-diameter aluminum shafts have traditionally been fletched with three 5-inch vanes or feathers. Smaller-diameter carbon shafts, which are also generally tipped with small- to average-diameter broadheads, are generally fletched with three 4-inch fletches.

There are three ways to position fletching onto the shaft: straight, offset and helical.

Most hunters position their fletching slightly offset. On both aluminum and carbon shafts using standard-diameter broadheads (no more than 1¹/₄ inches in diameter), an offset of just one or two degrees is enough. Full helical fletching, which presents difficulties in achieving arrow rest clearance, will unnecessarily rotate the shaft more quickly.

Should fletching be offset to the left or right? With plastic vanes, it doesn't matter a whit. With feathers, it depends on the wing of the bird—you must offset right-winged fletching to the right and left-wing fletching to the left. Also, some archers believe that the cock vane of the fletching should align perfectly with one of the blades of the broadhead for improved flight. I've experimented with this a lot over the years and have found that broadhead blade position in relation to my fletching makes no noticeable difference in accuracy.

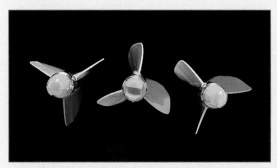

(From left) Straight, helical, offset fletching.

avoid—will withstand more shots than you can give an arrow before you lose or break it. You can pull your shafts from the target by grabbing the vanes without fearing damage. Vanes are also a bit quieter than feathers, especially if you accidentally rake them against brush or tree trunks and limbs.

Most target archers and bowhunters use plastic vanes today, but some still prefer natural feather fletching. Feathers are more forgiving than vanes, meaning that if minor contact with the arrow rest or bow riser occurs during the shot, feathers will ride over the contact point without noticeably steering the shaft off course. This is one reason feathers remain so popular with traditional archers. Though the difference is negligible, feathers also produce slightly faster arrow flight than vanes. Those who prefer feathers sometimes use special powders that help keep feathers impervious to wet weather.

Internal adapter (top); swaging (bottom).

ARROW POINT ADAPTERS

You can attach arrow points to the shaft one of two basic ways. The first is by "swaging" or gluing them on over the tapered shaft end. The second is to use a threaded adapter, which allows you to screw the point in and out as needed.

Swaging

Swaging is the old way to do things, though some archers still do it. They like the fact that they do not have to add the extra weight of an adapter to their shaft and that the glued-on point will not inadvertently come loose. However, using a point adapter is much more convenient.

Adapters

Modern aluminum shafts use an internal adapter, or insert, that is fitted securely into the shaft. Small-diameter carbon shafts use an external adapter, commonly called an "outsert," that you glue on over the shaft. Larger-diameter carbon arrows use inserts. Arrow inserts are made from either aluminum or carbon. When you're attaching adapters, you must put them on the shaft perfectly straight. Failure to do so results in a broadhead that points off-center, which will obviously steer the shaft off course.

Examples of good and poor feather fletching.

WOODEN ARROWS

Wooden arrow shafts have been around since the first primitive archer stalked his first prehistoric animal. But today, a bowhunter who uses wooden shafts is as rare as finding a needle in a haystack. The reason is simple: Manufacturers using space-age materials like aluminum and carbon can produce a superior product at less expense. Today, only a small number of low-volume manufacturers specialize in the craft of producing top-quality wooden shafts.

Still, wooden shafts live on in the hearts and souls of many traditional archers who find it sacrilegious to use anything but the same material used by archers and bowhunters of yesteryear.

WHAT KIND OF WOOD?

Down through history, just about every type of wood imaginable has been tried and used to make arrow shafts. English longbowmen used ash and

oak. Many American Indians used what is known in bowhunting circles as "natural" shafts, crafted from river cane and the small saplings of hazel, chokecherry and dogwood trees. Saxton Pope and Art Young, for whom the Pope and Young Club was named, preferred birch. The legendary Ishi used shafts made from hazel wood.

Today, the favored wood for arrow shafts is Port Orford white cedar. (Note: Not all cedar wood makes good arrow shafts.) The demand for the wooden dowels used to make shafts from this cedar was once so great that the company who produced the dowels, Rose City Wood Products, couldn't keep up. That prompted wooden arrow makers to turn to other woods—Douglas fir, Sitka spruce, yellow birch, Western larch, ironwood and white ash, among others—which they did while producing excellent wooden arrow shafts. The late Jay Massey, an Alaska hunting guide and traditional bowhunter par excellence, noted in his classic book, *The Traditional Bowyer's Bible*, that 24 different wood types have been, or are being, used to make wooden arrow shafts in North America.

THE TROUBLE WITH WOOD

One of the biggest problems with using wooden arrows is the lack of uniformity of each individual wooden dowel. Wood, by its nature, varies widely in weight and density. Putting together a dozen wooden arrows that weigh the same and have the same spine can take some time. And it is tough to find wooden shafts that are perfectly straight.

Wooden shafts will also warp in wet weather. Straightening them is a time-consuming process that requires experience. Wooden arrows simply will not last nearly as long as aluminum or carbon shafts; a weaker material, wood will crack or break much more quickly. In addition, repeatedly shooting with the same wooden shafts purportedly weakens their spines, changing the way they fly.

Top-quality wooden shafts cost as much or more than the best aluminum arrows. Though you can indeed find inexpensive wooden shafts, you should leave them to the casual plinker.

ATTACHING NOCKS AND BROADHEADS

Wooden arrows are not fitted with the same screw-in adapters that aluminum and carbon shafts are. Therefore, arrow points and nocks must be glued on, usually by swaging the shaft. AMO defines swaging as "the tapered shaping of an arrow foreshaft to directly accept an arrow point, commonly 5 degrees," or "the tapered shaping of an arrow rearshaft to directly accept an arrow nock, commonly $11^{1}/_{2}$ degrees."

As is the case with all arrow shafts, you must affix both the nock and

broadhead perfectly straight to achieve dart-like arrow flight.

FROM WHICH BOWS CAN I SHOOT WOODEN SHAFTS?

Naturally, wooden arrows are best served when shot from a traditional bow, either a recurve or longbow. Surprisingly, matching a set of wooden shafts to a longbow is more difficult than

Hunting with wooden shafts is grounded in tradition and challenge.

Arrow Shafts

Wood shafts worked for our forefathers and continue to work for hunters today.

matching to a recurve. A larger number of arrow spines and weights can be shot from a specific recurve than from a comparable longbow. Be that as it may, wooden shafts go hand in hand with traditional bows.

Despite the myth that you cannot shoot a wooden shaft from a compound bow, if you select a wooden shaft of the proper length, weight and spine for the compound bow, you can shoot it safely and accurately. The high-speed performance of a modern compound bow, however, makes them exceedingly tough on the relatively fragile wooden shafts. Following each and every shot, you must check wooden shafts over closely for cracks, dings and other structural problems, which could cause a wooden arrow to break or splinter upon the release of the next shot.

The finest wooden arrows are works of art, featuring a beautiful wood that's attractive and smells wonderful, especially when you're working with it. Many wooden shafts feature colorful cresting and a brilliant fletching. They look good and fly well too. Their effectiveness on game has been proven for centuries. If you decide that wood is for you, just be sure to take the time to select shafts carefully so that they match as closely as possible in length, weight and spine. That's the only way to ensure a quiver full of shafts that fly where you want them to on your next bowhunting adventure.

ALUMINUM ARROWS

The history of archery, and of bowhunting, is filled with the introduction of innovative new products. Some have had a marginal impact on the sport, while others have changed its face forever. With the exception of the compound bow, few archery innovations have impacted archery and bowhunting like the aluminum arrow shaft.

With the advent of aluminum arrows, archers could quickly find the right shaft for their specific requirements. It became easy to find all the arrows they wanted that were consistently straight, had a consistent spine and were extremely rugged. Aluminum shafts were relatively easy to work with too, making building arrows to specific requirements from individual shaft blanks a snap.

Doug Easton, a San Francisco Bay area bowhunter, introduced the first aluminum arrows to modern archery.

THE EASTON STORY

Doug Easton lived in the San Francisco Bay area in the late 1920s, where he was an avid bowhunter and equipment tinkerer who made high-quality cedar arrows. After moving to Los Angeles in 1932, Easton began experimenting with alternative shaft materials. The first Easton aluminum shafts were produced in 1939.

World War II slowed Easton's progress, but after the war, he stepped it up. He soon developed a process of drawing 1-inch aluminum tubing down to the desired shaft size and continued improving shaft quality using thermal and work-hardening processes. This led to the first trademarked aluminum arrow, the 24SRT-X. By 1948, Easton was producing 16 stock sizes of aluminum arrows.

In the early 1950s, Easton created the now-

Arrow Shafts

standard system of labeling arrow shaft sizes, where the first two numbers represent the shaft diameter in sixty-fourths of an inch and the second two numbers indicate the shaft wall thickness in thousandths of an inch. The Easton XX75, introduced in 1958, was available in an amazing 22 different sizes. The company continued to grow and moved to a new plant in Van Nuys, California, in the late 1960s.

By the late 1960s and early 1970s, the Easton company began making other aluminum products, including baseball and softball bats, hockey sticks, ski poles, bike frame tubing, backpack tent tubes and golf equipment, in addition to their now-famous arrow shafts. On December 31, 1972—the year marking the company's 50th anniversary —Doug Easton passed away. He had seen his one-man operation grow to a company with 120 employees. His vision had changed the history of the sport he loved.

Under the direction of Easton's son, Jim, the company continued to grow. In the mid-1980s Easton expanded its operation to include a modern manufacturing facility in Salt Lake City, Utah, which today houses one of the largest aluminum anodizing operations in the country.

In the early 1980s Easton introduced the then-radical concept of wrapping a thin-walled aluminum core with layers of lightweight, high-strength carbon fiber. The result was an extremely strong, stiff, lightweight and durable arrow shaft. By 1984 the first of its kind was used by Olympic archers to capture gold and silver medals. This concept lives on today in the form of the A/C/C, A/C/E and Hyper-Speed shafts. In 1991 Easton introduced the XX78 Super Slam aluminum arrow shaft system, featuring new camouflage patterns and processes, a new adjustable nock system and new methods of drawing aluminum tubing to thinner wall thickness with extreme consistency.

Easton aluminum arrows still dominate the market in terms of overall sales, partly because of their value. According to figures supplied by Easton, a single GameGetter aluminum arrow shaft in 1999 actually costs less than it did 20 years ago. Back then, the shaft cost about $1.47, while today it costs about $1.60. Considering inflation, it's about 45 percent cheaper today.

Choosing the Right Aluminum Shaft

There are so many different sizes of aluminum arrows out there today that selecting exactly the

As arrow shafts have become lighter, Easton's A/C/C arrow diameters are smaller and XX78 walls are thinner than ever.

A good archery shop will have large selection of aluminum arrows to choose from.

right shaft for your specific bowhunting needs can be somewhat confusing.

Most important, you need to choose a shaft with the correct spine. AMO defines spine as "the amount of bend (deflection) in an arrow shaft that is caused by a specific weight being placed at the center of the shaft, while the shaft is supported at a designated span; the recovery characteristic of an arrow that permits it to bend and then recover to its original shape in flight."

This definition refers to the fact that when you shoot an arrow shaft from the bow, it does not leave the bow perfectly straight. In fact, high-speed photography shows that the arrow bends an amazing amount as it leaves the bowstring, recovering to its original straight shape several yards downrange. Shafts released using a mechanical release aid tend to flex in a vertical (up and down) plane, while those released with fingers tend to flex in a horizontal (side to side) plane. A shaft of correct spine for a given bow will flex less and recover more quickly than one of improper spine, a critical factor in accurate arrow flight.

How do you go about selecting the correct spine for your bow? First, look at the Easton Arrow Shaft Selection Chart on the next two pages. The chart not only lists the many different sizes of alu-

minum shafts that will shoot well from your bow, but it also shows how to adjust the chart to take into account your type of bow, its wheels or cams and your draw weight and draw length. Using this chart takes the guesswork out of finding the right shaft size and spine for your bow.

In addition to selecting the correct spine, you must also make a decision concerning arrow weight. All things being equal, lightweight arrows will produce more initial raw arrow speed and a flatter trajectory than heavier arrows with a similar spine. However, lighter arrows generally have thinner walls, which makes them less durable. Also, heavier shafts will produce more kinetic energy, which helps penetration. Both shaft wall thickness and shaft diameter affect the shaft's spine, with the diameter having the greatest overall influence. Thus, a larger-diameter arrow with a thin wall can be made stiffer and lighter than a smaller-diameter arrow with a thick wall. For example, a 30 inch 2315 aluminum shaft, with a diameter of $^{23}/_{64}$ inch and wall thickness of $^{16}/_{1000}$ inch, weighs 350 grains, while a 30-inch 2413, with a diameter of $^{23}/_{64}$ inch and wall thickness of $^{13}/_{1000}$ inch, weighs 312 grains. Both have a comparable spine, yet the heavier of the two outweighs the other by 11 percent.

Arrow Selection Chart—Compound Bows

COMPOUND BOW
Release Aid
Actual or Calculated **PEAK BOW WEIGHT-LBS.**

Bowhunting with A/C/C® and HyperSpeed™
Carbon arrows may be used for hunting if special precautions are taken. See your dealer or the Easton information packed with A/C/C or HyperSpeed shafts.

Correct Arrow Length for Hunting

ROUND WHEEL — Broadhead or Field Point Wt. Only				SOFT CAM — Broadhead or Field Point Wt. Only				HARD CAM (Speed Cam) — Broadhead or Field Point Wt. Only				22½" **23"** -23½" (Size / Model / Weight)	23½" **24"** -24½" (Size / Model / Weight)	24½" **25"** -25½" (Size / Model / Weight)	25½" **26"** -26½" (Size / Model / Weight)
75 (grains) 65-85	100 (grains) 90-110	125 (grains) 115-135	150 (grains) 140-160	75 (grains) 65-85	100 (grains) 90-110	125 (grains) 115-135	150 (grains) 140-160	75 (grains) 65-85	100 (grains) 90-110	125 (grains) 115-135	150 (grains) 140-160				
50 TO 55	47 TO 52	44 TO 49	41 TO 46	45 TO 50	42 TO 47	39 TO 44	36 TO 41	40 TO 45	37 TO 42	34 TO 39	31 TO 36		1813 / 75 / 189 1716 / 75 / 217	1913 / 75 / 209 A 1816 / 75 / 232 B	2012, **1913** / X7, **75** / 208 A, **217 B** 1816 / 75 / 241 C
55 TO 60	52 TO 57	49 TO 54	46 TO 51	50 TO 55	47 TO 52	44 TO 49	41 TO 46	45 TO 50	42 TO 47	39 TO 44	36 TO 41	1813 / 75 / 181 1716 / 75 / 208	1913 / 75 / 200 A 1816 / 75 / 223 B	2012, **1913** / X7, **75** / 200 A, **209 B** 1816 / 75 / 232 C 3L-18, 2L-18 / A/C/C, HSpd / 194, 148	2012, 2013 / X7, 75 / 208 B, 234 A 1916 / 75 / 261 A
60 TO 65	57 TO 62	54 TO 59	51 TO 56	55 TO 60	52 TO 57	49 TO 54	46 TO 51	50 TO 55	47 TO 52	44 TO 49	41 TO 46	1913 / 75 / 192 A 1816 / 75 / 213 B	2012, **1913** / X7, **75** / 192 A, **200 B** 1816 / 75 / 223 C	2012, 2013 / X7, 75 / 200 B, 225 A 1916 / 75 / 251 A 3L-18, 2L-18 / A/C/C, HSpd / 186, 142	2112, **2013** / X7, **75** / 219 A, **234 B** 1916 / 75 / 261 B 3L-18, 2L-18 / A/C/C, HSpd / 194, 148
65 TO 70	62 TO 67	59 TO 64	56 TO 61	60 TO 65	57 TO 62	54 TO 59	51 TO 56	55 TO 60	52 TO 57	49 TO 54	46 TO 51	2012, **1913** / X7, **75** / 184 A, **192 B** 1816 / 75 / 213 C	2012, 2013 / X7, 75 / 192 B, 216 A 1916 / 75 / 241 A 3L-18, 2L-18 / A/C/C, HSpd / 179, 137	2112, **2013** / X7, **75** / 210 A, **225 B** 1916 / 75 / 251 B 3L-18, 2L-18 / A/C/C, HSpd / 186, 142	2112, 2113 / X7, 75 / 219 B, 242 A 2016 / S,75 / 275 A 3-18, 2-18 / A/C/C, HSpd / 203, 161
70 TO 76	67 TO 73	64 TO 70	61 TO 67	65 TO 70	62 TO 67	59 TO 64	56 TO 61	60 TO 65	57 TO 62	54 TO 59	51 TO 56	2012, 2013 / X7, 75 / 184 B, 207 A 1916 / 75 / 231 A 3L-18, 2L-18 / A/C/C, HSpd / 172, 131	2112, **2013** / X7, **75** / 202 A, **216 B** 1916 / 75 / 241 B 3L-18, 2L-18 / A/C/C, HSpd / 179, 137	2112, 2113 / X7, 75 / 210 B, 233 A 2016 / S,75 / 264 A 3-18, 2-18 / A/C/C, HSpd / 195, 155	2212, **2114**, 2016, 2115, **2018** / S, **S,75**, S,75, S,75, **S,75,E** / 230 B, **256 B**, 275 C, 280 A, **319 A** 3-28, 2-28 / A/C/C, HSpd / 211, 170
76 TO 82	73 TO 79	70 TO 76	67 TO 73	70 TO 76	67 TO 73	64 TO 70	61 TO 67	65 TO 70	62 TO 67	59 TO 64	56 TO 61	2112, **2013** / X7, **75** / 194 A, **207 B** 1916 / 75 / 231 B 3L-18, 2L-18 / A/C/C, HSpd / 172, 131	2112, 2113 / X7, 75 / 202 B, 223 A 2016 / S,75 / 253 A 3-18, 2-18 / A/C/C, HSpd / 187, 149	2212, **2114**, 2016, 2115, **2018** / S, **S,75**, S,75, S,75, **S,75,E** / 221 B, **247 B**, 264 C, 269 A, **307 A** 3-28, 2-28 / A/C/C, HSpd / 203, 163	2212, 2114, 2115, 2018 / S, S,75, S,75, S,75,E / 230 C, 256 C, 280 B, 319 B 3-28, 2-28 / A/C/C, HSpd / 211, 170
82 TO 88	79 TO 85	76 TO 82	73 TO 79	76 TO 82	73 TO 79	70 TO 76	67 TO 73	70 TO 76	67 TO 73	64 TO 70	61 TO 67	2112, 2113 / X7, 75 / 194 B, 214 A 2016 / S,75 / 243 A 3-18, 2-18 / A/C/C, HSpd / 180, 143	2212, **2114**, 2016, 2115, **2018** / S, **S,75**, S,75, S,75, **S,75,E** / 212 B, **237 B**, 253 C, 259 A, **295 A** 3-28, 2-28 / A/C/C, HSpd / 194, 157	2212, **2213**, 2114, 2115, **2018** / S, **S,75**, S,75, S,75, **S,75,E** / 221 B, **246 A**, 247 C, 269 B, **307 B** 3-28, 2-28 / A/C/C, HSpd / 203, 163	2312, 2213, 2215, 2117 / S, S,75, S,75, S,75,E / 246 B, 256 C, 277 B, 313 A 3-39, 2-39 / A/C/C, HSpd / 223, 180
88 TO 94	85 TO 91	82 TO 88	79 TO 85	82 TO 88	79 TO 85	76 TO 82	73 TO 79	76 TO 82	73 TO 79	70 TO 76	67 TO 73	2212, **2114**, 2016, 2115, **2018** / S, **S,75**, S,75, S,75, **S,75,E** / 203 B, **227 B**, 243 C, 248 B, **282 A** 3-28, 2-28 / A/C/C, HSpd / 186, 150	2212, **2213**, 2114, 2115, **2018** / S, **S,75**, S,75, S,75, **S,75,E** / 212 C, **236 A**, 237 C, 259 B, **295 B** 3-28, 2-28 / A/C/C, HSpd / 194, 157	2312, 2314, **2215**, 2117 / S, S,75, **S,75**, S,75,E / 237 B, 246 C, **267 B**, 301 A 3-39, 2-39 / A/C/C, HSpd / 215, 173	2412, **2314**, 2215, 2117, **2216** / S, **S,75**, S,75, S,75,E, **S,75** / 251 A, **277 A**, 277 C, 313 B, **313 A** 3-49, 2-49 / A/C/C, HSpd / 230, 186
94 TO 100	91 TO 97	88 TO 94	85 TO 91	88 TO 94	85 TO 91	82 TO 88	79 TO 85	82 TO 88	79 TO 85	76 TO 82	73 TO 79	2212, **2213**, 2114, 2115, **2018** / S, **S,75**, S,75, S,75, **S,75,E** / 203 C, **226 A**, 227 C, 248 B, **282 B** 3-28, 2-28 / A/C/C, HSpd / 186, 150	2312, 2213, **2215**, 2117 / S, S,75, **S,75**, S,75,E / 228 B, 236 C, **256 B**, 289 A 3-39, 2-39 / A/C/C, HSpd / 206, 166	2412, 2314, **2215**, 2117, **2216** / S, S,75, **S,75**, S,75,E, **S,75** / 241 A, 266 A, **267 C**, 301 B, **301 A** 3-49, 2-49 / A/C/C, HSpd / 221, 179	**2413**, 2314, **2315**, 2216, 2219 / **S,75**, S,75, **S,75**, S,75, S,75,E / **270 A**, 277 B, **303 B**, 313 B, 358 A 3-49, 2-49 / A/C/C, HSpd / 230, 186
100 TO 106	97 TO 103	94 TO 100	91 TO 97	94 TO 100	91 TO 97	88 TO 94	85 TO 91	88 TO 94	85 TO 91	82 TO 88	79 TO 85	2312, 2213, **2215**, **2117** / S, S,75, **S,75**, **S,75,E** / 218 B, 226 B, **245 B**, **277 A** 3-39, 2-39 / A/C/C, HSpd / 197, 159	2412, **2314**, 2215, 2117, **2216** / S, **S,75**, S,75, S,75,E, **S,75** / 232 A, **255 A**, 256 C, 289 B, **289 A** 3-49, 2-49 / A/C/C, HSpd / 212, 172	**2413**, **2315**, 2216, **2219** / **S,75**, **S,75**, S,75, **S,75,E** / **260 A**, **292 A**, 301 B, **344 A** 3-49, 2-49 / A/C/C, HSpd / 221, 179	2512, 2413, **2315**, 2415, **2219** / S, S,75, **S,75**, S, **S,75,E** / 267 A, 270 B, **303 B**, 318 A, **358 B** 3-60, 2-60 / A/C/C, HSpd / 246, 192
106 TO 112	103 TO 109	100 TO 106	97 TO 103	100 TO 106	97 TO 103	94 TO 100	91 TO 97	94 TO 100	91 TO 97	88 TO 94	85 TO 91	2412, **2314**, 2215, 2117, **2216** / S, **S,75**, S,75, S,75,E, **S,75** / 222 A, **244 A**, 245 C, 277 B, **277 A** 3-49, 2-49 / A/C/C, HSpd / 203, 165	**2413**, 2314, **2315**, 2216, 2219 / **S,75**, S,75, **S,75**, S,75, S,75,E / **250 A**, 255 B, **280 A**, 289 B, 329 A 3-49, 2-49 / A/C/C, HSpd / 212, 172	2512, 2413, **2315**, 2415, **2219** / S, S,75, **S,75**, S, **S,75,E** / 257 A, 260 B, **292 B**, 306 A, **344 B** 3-60, 2-60 / A/C/C, HSpd / 236, 185	2512, **2315**, 2415, **2219** / S, **S,75**, S, **S,75,E** / 267 A, **303 B**, 318 A, **358 B** 3-60, 2-60 / A/C/C, HSpd / 246, 192

Easton Hunting Shaft Size Selection Chart

This chart was set up using: • Recurve bows with finger release • High-performance, 65% AMO letoff compound bows with release aids • Fast Flight® strings. If your equipment is set up differently, see the "Variables" section to determine your **Calculated Peak Bow Weight** before using this chart.

RECURVE BOW Finger Release — Actual or Calculated **PEAK BOW WEIGHT-LBS**

Correct Arrow Length for Hunting

Column key for each arrow-length group: **Shaft Size · Shaft Model · Shaft Weight**

Peak Bow Weight columns (Broadhead or Field Point Wt. Only): **75 gr (65-85) · 100 gr (90-110) · 125 gr (115-135) · 150 gr (140-160)**

Peak Bow Weight — 75: 35-40 / 100: 32-37 / 125: 29-34 / 150: 26-31

Arrow Length	Shaft Size	Shaft Model	Shaft Weight
27"	2012	X7	216 B
27"	2013	75	243 A
27"	1916	75	271 B
27"	3L-18	A/C/C	201
27"	2L-18	HSpd	154
28"	2112	X7	236 A
28"	2013	75	252 B
28"	1916	75	281 B
28"	3L-18	A/C/C	209
28"	2L-18	HSpd	159
29"	2112	X7	244 B
29"	2113	75	270 A
29"	2016	S,75	306 A
29"	3-18	A/C/C	226
29"	2-18	HSpd	180
30"	2212	S	265 B
30"	2114	S,75	296 B
30"	2016	S,75	317 C
30"	2115	S,75	323 A
30"	2018	S,75,E	368 A
30"	3-28	A/C/C	243
30"	2-28	HSpd	196
31"	2212	S	274 C
31"	2213	S,75	305 A
31"	2114	S,75	306 C
31"	2115	S,75	334 B
31"	2018	S,75,E	381 B
31"	3-39	A/C/C	275
31"	2-39	HSpd	221
32"	2312	S	303 B
32"	2213	S,75	315 C
32"	2215	S,75	341 B
32"	2117	S,75,E	385 A
32"	3-49	A/C/C	291
32"	2-49	HSpd	236
33"	2412	S	318 A
33"	2314	S,75	351 A
33"	2215	S,75	352 C
33"	2117	S,75,E	397 B
33"	2216	S,75	397 A
33"	3-49	A/C/C	291
33"	2-49	HSpd	236

Peak Bow Weight — 75: 40-45 / 100: 37-42 / 125: 34-39 / 150: 31-36

Arrow Length	Shaft Size	Shaft Model	Shaft Weight
27"	2112	X7	227 A
27"	2013	75	243 B
27"	1916	75	271 B
27"	3L-18	A/C/C	201
27"	2L-18	HSpd	154
28"	2112	X7	236 B
28"	2113	75	260 A
28"	2016	S,75	296 A
28"	3-18	A/C/C	219
28"	2-18	HSpd	174
29"	2212	S	256 B
29"	2114	S,75	286 B
29"	2016	S,75	306 C
29"	2115	S,75	312 A
29"	2018	S,75,E	356 A
29"	3-28	A/C/C	235
29"	2-28	HSpd	189
30"	2212	S	265 C
30"	2213	S,75	295 A
30"	2114	S,75	296 C
30"	2115	S,75	323 B
30"	2018	S,75,E	368 B
30"	3-28	A/C/C	243
30"	2-28	HSpd	196
31"	2312	S	294 B
31"	2213	S,75	305 C
31"	2215	S,75	331 B
31"	2117	S,75,E	373 A
31"	3-39	A/C/C	266
31"	2-39	HSpd	215
32"	2412	S	309 A
32"	2314	S,75	341 A
32"	2215	S,75	341 C
32"	2117	S,75,E	385 B
32"	2216	S,75	385 A
32"	3-49	A/C/C	283
32"	2-49	HSpd	229
33"	2413	S,75	343 A
33"	2314	S,75	351 B
33"	2315	S,75	385 A
33"	2216	S,75	397 B
33"	2219	S,75,E	454 A
33"	3-49	A/C/C	291
33"	2-49	HSpd	236

Peak Bow Weight — 75: 45-50 / 100: 42-47 / 125: 39-44 / 150: 36-41

Arrow Length	Shaft Size	Shaft Model	Shaft Weight
27"	2112	X7	227 B
27"	2113	75	251 A
27"	2016	S,75	285 A
27"	3-18	A/C/C	211
27"	2-18	HSpd	168
28"	2212	S	248 B
28"	2114	S,75	276 B
28"	2016	S,75	296 C
28"	2115	S,75	302 A
28"	2018	S,75,E	344 A
28"	3-28	A/C/C	227
28"	2-28	HSpd	183
29"	2212	S	256 C
29"	2213	S,75	285 A
29"	2114	S,75	286 C
29"	2115	S,75	312 B
29"	2018	S,75,E	356 B
29"	3-28	A/C/C	235
29"	2-28	HSpd	189
30"	2312	S	284 B
30"	2213	S,75	295 C
30"	2215	S,75	320 B
30"	2117	S,75,E	361 A
30"	3-39	A/C/C	257
30"	2-39	HSpd	208
31"	2412	S	299 A
31"	2314	S,75	330 A
31"	2215	S,75	331 C
31"	2117	S,75,E	373 B
31"	2216	S,75	373 A
31"	3-49	A/C/C	274
31"	2-49	HSpd	222
32"	2413	S,75	333 A
32"	2314	S,75	341 B
32"	2315	S,75	373 B
32"	2216	S,75	385 B
32"	2219	S,75,E	441 A
32"	3-49	A/C/C	283
32"	2-49	HSpd	229
33"	2512	S	339 A
33"	2413	S,75	343 B
33"	2315	S,75	385 B
33"	2415	S	404 A
33"	2219	S,75,E	454 B
33"	3-60	A/C/C	312
33"	2-60	HSpd	244

Peak Bow Weight — 75: 50-55 / 100: 47-52 / 125: 44-49 / 150: 41-46

Arrow Length	Shaft Size	Shaft Model	Shaft Weight
27"	2212	S	239 B
27"	2114	S,75	266 B
27"	2016	S,75	285 C
27"	2115	S,75	291 A
27"	2018	S,75,E	332 A
27"	3-28	A/C/C	219
27"	2-28	HSpd	176
28"	2212	S	248 C
28"	2213	S,75	275 A
28"	2114	S,75	275 C
28"	2115	S,75	302 B
28"	2018	S,75,E	344 B
28"	3-28	A/C/C	227
28"	2-28	HSpd	183
29"	2312	S	275 B
29"	2213	S,75	285 C
29"	2215	S,75	309 B
29"	2117	S,75,E	349 A
29"	3-39	A/C/C	249
29"	2-39	HSpd	201
30"	2412	S	290 A
30"	2314	S,75	319 A
30"	2215	S,75	320 C
30"	2117	S,75,E	361 B
30"	2216	S,75	361 A
30"	3-49	A/C/C	265
30"	2-49	HSpd	215
31"	2413	S,75	322 A
31"	2314	S,75	330 B
31"	2315	S,75	362 A
31"	2216	S,75	373 B
31"	2219	S,75,E	427 A
31"	3-49	A/C/C	274
31"	2-49	HSpd	222
32"	2512	S	329 A
32"	2413	S,75	333 B
32"	2315	S,75	373 B
32"	2415	S	392 A
32"	2219	S,75,E	441 B
32"	3-60	A/C/C	302
32"	2-60	HSpd	236
33"	2512	S	339 A
33"	2315	S,75	385 B
33"	2415	S	404 A
33"	2219	S,75,E	454 B
33"	3-60	A/C/C	312
33"	2-60	HSpd	244

Peak Bow Weight — 75: 55-60 / 100: 52-57 / 125: 49-54 / 150: 46-51

Arrow Length	Shaft Size	Shaft Model	Shaft Weight
27"	2212	S	239 C
27"	2213	S,75	265 A
27"	2114	S,75	266 C
27"	2115	S,75	291 B
27"	2018	S,75,E	332 B
27"	3-28	A/C/C	219
27"	2-28	HSpd	176
28"	2312	S	265 B
28"	2213	S,75	275 C
28"	2215	S,75	299 B
28"	2117	S,75,E	337 A
28"	3-39	A/C/C	240
28"	2-39	HSpd	194
29"	2412	S	280 A
29"	2314	S,75	309 A
29"	2215	S,75	309 C
29"	2117	S,75,E	349 B
29"	2216	S,75	349 A
29"	3-49	A/C/C	256
29"	2-49	HSpd	208
30"	2413	S,75	312 A
30"	2314	S,75	319 B
30"	2315	S,75	350 A
30"	2216	S,75	361 B
30"	2219	S,75,E	413 A
30"	3-49	A/C/C	265
30"	2-49	HSpd	215
31"	2512	S	318 A
31"	2413	S,75	322 B
31"	2315	S,75	362 B
31"	2415	S	379 A
31"	2219	S,75,E	427 B
31"	3-60	A/C/C	293
31"	2-60	HSpd	229
32"	2512	S	329 A
32"	2315	S,75	373 B
32"	2415	S	392 A
32"	2219	S,75,E	441 B
32"	3-60	A/C/C	302
32"	2-60	HSpd	236
33"	2512	S	339 B
33"	2514	S,75	374 A
33"	2317	S,75	438 A
33"	3-71	A/C/C	327
33"	2-71	HSpd	265

Peak Bow Weight — 75: 60-65 / 100: 57-62 / 125: 54-59 / 150: 51-56

Arrow Length	Shaft Size	Shaft Model	Shaft Weight
27"	2312	S	256 B
27"	2213	S,75	265 C
27"	2215	S,75	288 B
27"	2117	S,75,E	325 A
27"	3-39	A/C/C	232
27"	2-39	HSpd	187
28"	2412	S	270 A
28"	2314	S,75	298 A
28"	2215	S,75	299 C
28"	2117	S,75,E	337 B
28"	2216	S,75	337 A
28"	3-49	A/C/C	247
28"	2-49	HSpd	200
29"	2413	S,75	302 A
29"	2314	S,75	309 B
29"	2315	S,75	338 A
29"	2216	S,75	349 B
29"	2219	S,75,E	399 A
29"	3-49	A/C/C	256
29"	2-49	HSpd	208
30"	2512	S	308 A
30"	2413	S,75	312 B
30"	2315	S,75	350 B
30"	2415	S	367 A
30"	2219	S,75,E	413 B
30"	3-60	A/C/C	284
30"	2-60	HSpd	221
31"	2512	S	318 A
31"	2315	S,75	362 B
31"	2415	S	379 A
31"	2219	S,75,E	427 B
31"	3-71	A/C/C	317
31"	2-71	HSpd	257
32"	2512	S	329 B
32"	2514	S,75	363 A
32"	2317	S,75	424 A
32"	3-71	A/C/C	317
32"	2-71	HSpd	257
33"	2514	S	374 B
33"	2613	S	379 A
33"	2317	S	438 B
33"	2419	75	480 A
33"	3-71	A/C/C	327
33"	2-71	HSpd	265

Peak Bow Weight — 75: 65-70 / 100: 62-67 / 125: 59-64 / 150: 56-61

Arrow Length	Shaft Size	Shaft Model	Shaft Weight
27"	2412	S	261 A
27"	2314	S,75	287 A
27"	2215	S,75	288 C
27"	2117	S,75,E	325 B
27"	2216	S,75	325 A
27"	3-49	A/C/C	238
27"	2-49	HSpd	193
28"	2413	S,75	291 A
28"	2314	S,75	298 B
28"	2315	S,75	327 A
28"	2216	S,75	337 B
28"	2219	S,75,E	386 A
28"	3-49	A/C/C	247
28"	2-49	HSpd	200
29"	2512	S	298 A
29"	2413	S,75	302 B
29"	2315	S,75	338 B
29"	2415	S	355 A
29"	2219	S,75,E	399 B
29"	3-60	A/C/C	274
29"	2-60	HSpd	214
30"	2512	S	308 A
30"	2315	S,75	350 B
30"	2415	S	367 A
30"	2219	S,75,E	413 B
30"	3-60	A/C/C	284
30"	2-60	HSpd	221
31"	2512	S	318 B
31"	2514	S,75	351 A
31"	2317	S,75	411 A
31"	2419	75	451 A
31"	3-71	A/C/C	308
31"	2-71	HSpd	249
32"	2514	S,75	363 B
32"	2613	S	368 A
32"	2317	S,75	424 B
32"	2419	75	466 A
32"	3-71	A/C/C	317
32"	2-71	HSpd	257
33"	2514	S,75	374 B
33"	2613	S	379 A
33"	2317	S,75	438 B
33"	2419	75	480 B
33"	3-71	A/C/C	327
33"	2-71	HSpd	265

Peak Bow Weight — 75: 70-76 / 100: 67-73 / 125: 64-70 / 150: 61-67

Arrow Length	Shaft Size	Shaft Model	Shaft Weight
27"	2413	S,75	281 A
27"	2314	S,75	287 B
27"	2315	S,75	315 A
27"	2216	S,75	325 B
27"	2219	S,75,E	372 A
27"	3-49	A/C/C	238
27"	2-49	HSpd	193
28"	2512	S	288 A
28"	2413	S,75	291 B
28"	2315	S,75	327 B
28"	2415	S	343 A
28"	2219	S,75,E	386 B
28"	3-60	A/C/C	265
28"	2-60	HSpd	207
29"	2512	S	298 A
29"	2315	S,75	338 B
29"	2415	S	355 A
29"	2219	S,75,E	399 B
29"	3-60	A/C/C	274
29"	2-60	HSpd	214
30"	2512	S	308 B
30"	2514	S,75	340 A
30"	2317	S,75	398 A
30"	3-71	A/C/C	298
30"	2-71	HSpd	241
31"	2514	S,75	351 B
31"	2613	S	356 A
31"	2317	S,75	411 B
31"	2419	75	451 A
31"	3-71	A/C/C	308
31"	2-71	HSpd	249
32"	2613	S	368 A
33"	2613	S	379 A

Peak Bow Weight — 75: 76-82 / 100: 73-79 / 125: 70-76 / 150: 67-73

Arrow Length	Shaft Size	Shaft Model	Shaft Weight
27"	2512	S	277 A
27"	2413	S,75	281 B
27"	2315	S,75	315 B
27"	2415	S	330 A
27"	2219	S,75,E	372 B
27"	3-60	A/C/C	255
27"	2-60	HSpd	199
28"	2512	S	288 B
28"	2514	S,75	329 A
28"	2317	S,75	371 A
28"	2419	75	422 A
28"	3-71	A/C/C	288
28"	2-71	HSpd	233
29"	2514	S,75	329 A
29"	2613	S	333 A
29"	2317	S,75	385 A
29"	2419	75	422 A
29"	3-71	A/C/C	288
29"	2-71	HSpd	233
30"	2514	S,75	340 B
30"	2613	S	345 A
30"	2317	S,75	398 B
30"	2419	75	437 A
30"	3-71	A/C/C	298
30"	2-71	HSpd	241
31"	2613	S	356 A
31"	2419	75	451 B
31"	3-71	A/C/C	308
31"	2-71	HSpd	249
32"	2613	S	368

Peak Bow Weight — 75: 82-88 / 100: 79-85 / 125: 76-82 / 150: 73-79

Arrow Length	Shaft Size	Shaft Model	Shaft Weight
27"	2512	S	277 A
27"	2315	S,75	315 B
27"	2415	S	330 A
27"	2219	S,75,E	372 B
27"	3-60	A/C/C	255
27"	2-60	HSpd	199
28"	2512	S	288 B
28"	2514	S,75	317 A
28"	2317	S,75	371 A
28"	2419	75	422 A
28"	3-71	A/C/C	288
28"	2-71	HSpd	233
29"	2514	S,75	329 B
29"	2613	S	333 A
29"	2317	S,75	385 B
29"	2419	75	422 A
29"	3-71	A/C/C	288
29"	2-71	HSpd	233
30"	2613	S	345 A
30"	2419	75	437 B
31"	2613	S	356

Peak Bow Weight — 75: 88-94 / 100: 85-91 / 125: 82-88 / 150: 79-85

Arrow Length	Shaft Size	Shaft Model	Shaft Weight
27"	2512	S	277 B
27"	2514	S,75	306 A
27"	2317	S,75	358 A
27"	3-71	A/C/C	268
27"	2-71	HSpd	217
28"	2514	S,75	317 B
28"	2613	S	322 A
28"	2317	S,75	371 B
28"	2419	75	407 A
28"	3-71	A/C/C	278
28"	2-71	HSpd	225
29"	2514	S,75	329 B
29"	2613	S	333 A
29"	2317	S,75	385 B
29"	2419	75	422 A
29"	3-71	A/C/C	288
29"	2-71	HSpd	233

WARNING: Over stressing compound bows by using arrows lighter than AMO recommendations may cause damage to the bow and possible injury to the shooter.

AMO compound bow manufacturers have issued the following warning:
• Total arrow weight (shaft weight shown in Easton chart plus weight of point, insert [if used] and fletching plus nock and UNI Bushing) should be greater than 6 grains per pound of peak bow weight for a 60# compound bow with a 30" draw length*.
• Bow weights lighter than 60# and draw lengths shorter than 30" can use arrows lighter than 6 grains/pound of peak bow weight*.
• Bow weights heavier than 60# and draw lengths longer than 30" should use arrows heavier than 6 grains/pound of peak bow weight*.

Weight-Forward Balance

People often overlook an arrow shaft's weight-forward balance (W/F), or front of center (FOC)—especially with broadheads—as a factor in accurate arrow flight. Weight-forward balance refers to the distance at which the shaft balances forward of its midpoint. Picture a set of balance scales. When you place equal weights in each pan, the scale balances. Properly built arrow shafts, rather than balancing at their midpoint, balance a bit forward of their center-line because of the relatively heavy arrow tip.

Having your shaft balance forward of the center point is important for proper arrow flight. Because of an arrow's arcing trajectory, having the balance point front of center helps keep the tip driving in a straight line as the arrow drives forward through the air. The proper balance point becomes even more critical when the shaft's fletching has to overcome the planing characteristics of broadhead blades as it steers the shaft on a true course.

Calculating Your Weight-Forward Balance

Weight-forward balance—usually expressed in a percentage—is easy to calculate. First, measure your shaft's length, from the end of the shaft to the notch on the arrow nock where it contacts the string. Say that's 30 inches. Divide that by two to get the center point of your shaft, or 15 inches. Mark this spot with a felt-tip pen.

Now place the shaft on the edge of your index finger, sliding it forward of the center point until it balances. This is the true balance point of your shaft. Mark this spot with the felt pen. Measure the distance between your two pen marks and write down the length. Say that's 3 inches. Divide this distance by overall shaft length and multiply by 100. This is your percentage of weight-forward balance, or front of center. In this case, it's 10 percent.

Generally, a W/F between 7 and 10 percent is the accepted standard for aluminum arrow shafts. In my experience, a W/F between 8 and 11 percent has always resulted in dart-like arrow flight and tight groups when I've been shooting aluminum arrows. However, I've also found that an exaggerated W/F from 10 to 15 percent seems to work best at times with small-diameter, lightweight carbon shafts.

You can control your weight-forward balance simply by switching to a heavier or lighter arrow point.

The Final Determination

There are several steps in putting together an accurate bow-and-arrow setup. These include matching the accessories to the bow, using perfectly straight, properly spined arrow shafts built with the right components and adequate fletching, making sure the fletch doesn't come in contact with the arrow rest or riser and meticulously paper-tuning. Still, you always make the final determination on the target range. Does this setup shoot those shafts into tight clusters at hunting distances?

If everything else is as it's supposed to be but your groups open up more than they should, check your W/F. Many speed-crazy bowhunters think that by scrimping on their broadhead weight they can squeeze a few extra fps out of their setups—which they can. But in doing so, they often compromise their W/F. In the long run, does speed matter if the result is erratic arrow flight?

As champion 3-D and indoor tournament shooter Randy Ulmer, who is also one whale of a bowhunter, likes to say, "I'd rather have a slow hit than a fast miss any day."

F.O.C. Calculations

$$\text{F.O.C. \%} = \frac{100 \times (A - L/2)}{L}$$

L = Correct Arrow Length—distance from bottom of nock groove to end of shaft

A = Distance from bottom of nock groove to balance position of finished arrow (including point, insert, nock and fletching)

L = Correct Arrow Length
Center of
Correct Arrow Length

F.O.C. Distance

½ Length = L/2

Front-of-Center balance position of the finished arrow

A

When setting up a new bow, I visit my local archery pro shop. There I use the shaft chart for recommendations and buy two completed arrows from the shop owner to try out. I paper-tune the bow with these shafts using the weight field point and/or broadhead I want to shoot to make sure they will tune with my bow. I then shoot them on the target range to make sure I can achieve the kinds of tight arrow groups at distances that satisfy me. If everything works well, I buy a dozen more arrows. If not, I start the process over with a different shaft size.

FUTURE TRENDS

Arrow shaft makers and archery retailers have identified that more of today's bowhunters are shooting more expensive shafts than ever before. The contemporary bowhunter wants the best shafts possible and will pay a few dollars more for top-of-the-line arrows. Along with this trend is a shift to using shafts with tunable components, especially tunable nocks.

So what's on the arrow shaft horizon? Only time will tell. But one thing's for certain—today's manufacturers are not standing still when it comes to shaft development.

Easton's Director of Marketing, Randy Schoeck, says that the company is doing anything but resting on its laurels. Instead, they continue to search for new materials that lend themselves to producing a better arrow shaft at a price that a great number of people can afford. Materials they've looked at in recent years include boron and Kevlar, but nothing has risen to the surface yet to take the place of aluminum and carbon shafts. "Right now, aluminum, aluminum-carbon composites and pure carbon are the only choices that offer reasonable performance values today," Schoeck maintains. "We are continuing to look, though, and if we can find something that will work better, we'll certainly use it."

Arrow Shaft Manufacturers

Beman USA
543 N. Neil Armstrong Rd.
Salt Lake City, UT 84116
(801) 363-2990

Carbon Impact
P.O. Box 1618
Acme, MI 49610
(616) 938-3099

Carbon Tech
9050 Ranchview Ct.
Elk Grove, CA 95624
(916) 755-3622

Custom Archery Equipment
21529 Menlo Ave.
Torrance, CA 90502
(310) 212-5500

Easton Technical Products
5040 W. Harold Gatty Dr.
Salt Lake City, UT 84116
(801) 539-1400

Game Tracker/AFC
3476 Eastman Dr.
Flushing, MI 48433
(810) 733-6360

Gold Tip Corporation
140 S. Main St.
Pleasant Grove, UT 84062
(800) 551-0541

True Flight Arrow Co.
Box 746
Monticello, IN 47960
(800) 348-2224

CARBON ARROWS

Aluminum has without question been the forerunner when it comes to arrow shaft material. Aluminum is still the market leader in terms of overall sales. Few bowhunters have considered that new shaft materials might challenge aluminum's dominance. But now there's a new kid on the block. Carbon (graphite) shafts have come on like gangbusters in recent years. Is carbon the shaft of the future?

THE CARBON ARROW ADVANTAGES

Carbon shaft sales continue to grow annually simply because they can provide several performance advantages over aluminum shafts.

Arrow Speed

One benefit is raw arrow speed, achieved because a carbon shaft of the same length and spine as a comparable aluminum shaft weighs less. "While the exact numbers vary, of course, we figure you get anywhere from 20 to 30 fps more from a carbon shaft than a comparable aluminum arrow," states Jeff McNail, Assistant Brand Manager at Beman, a respected manufacturer of carbon arrows.

Durability

Another advantage is durability. Carbon shafts are just plain tough, able to withstand much more abuse than aluminum and aluminum-carbon composite (A/C/C) arrows. With carbon, the shaft is either as straight as it came from the factory, or it's broken—they can't be bent—and it takes quite a wallop to break them. (When aluminum is involved, like with A/C/C, the shafts can bend, often imperceptibly, though you can straighten them.)

Penetration

And third, carbon shafts out-penetrate any other shaft on the market. While no empirical, scientifically valid research exists to back up this claim, after shooting a lot of aluminum, aluminum/carbon composite and pure carbon shafts into all sorts of targets—as well as into big-game animals including deer, hogs, elk, bears, muskox and more—in weather ranging from 100°F to minus 50°F, there's no question in my mind that carbon shafts offer the best penetration.

USING AND SELECTING CARBON ARROWS

Still, many pro shops don't stock or aggressively promote carbon shafts, which means that many bowhunters have not yet been exposed to them. In most cases, the dealers who do sell carbon arrows shoot carbon themselves and understand how to build quality carbon shafts as well as how to tune bows to shoot these small-diameter arrows.

"Using carbon shafts is a bit different than using an aluminum arrow," explains Jerry Fletcher, a very experienced bowhunter and also the 1998 state field archery champion and owner of Fletcher's Archery in Wasilla, Alaska. "For example, I've found that when tuning carbons, a 'perfect' paper tear isn't always the best in terms of the groups you'll shoot. Also, arrow rests that work well with aluminum arrows often don't work well with carbon shafts. And you sometimes need a bit more weight-forward balance with a carbon shaft than you do with aluminum to get consistently tight arrow groups at longer yardages with broadheads." Fletcher recommends a weight-

forward balance of 10 to 15 percent with carbon shafts. Jeff McNail of Beman, also an experienced tournament shooter and bowhunter, recommends a weight-forward balance of 9 to 12 percent with carbon arrows. The standard for aluminum arrows, on the other hand, is 7 to 10 percent.

Another advantage of carbon arrows is that a single shaft spine covers a much wider range of draw lengths and draw weights than comparable aluminum arrows do.

For example, most carbon arrow makers offer only three different spine sizes to cover the entire range of hunting bow draw length/draw weight combinations. For example, Beman's ICS Hunter shaft is available in just three spine sizes: 500, 400 and 340. One of these three arrow sizes will tune in bows ranging from 33 to 100 pounds of draw weight, and draw lengths between 23 and 33 inches, depending on the combination thereof. This makes it easy to select the right arrow shaft spine for your bow without worrying about being "on the cusp" of the right size. It also makes it easier for a pro shop to stock the right size shafts to take care of virtually all of its customers without having to carry dozens and dozens of different aluminum shaft spines in stock.

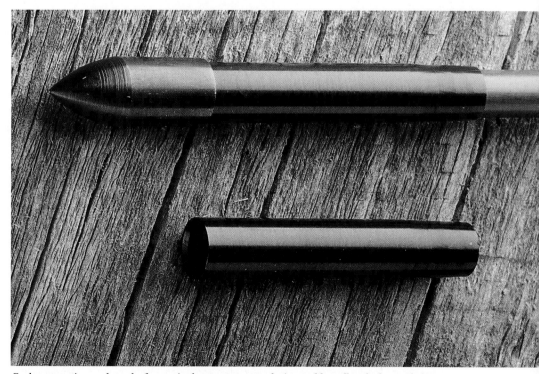

Early generation carbon shafts required outserts to attach tips and broadheads due to their smaller diameter.

Arrow Shafts

CARBON SHAFT PROBLEMS

Early-generation carbon shafts were so small in diameter that archers had to use an "outsert" to affix screw-on broadheads, field points and nocks. An outsert—a carbon component that glues on over the shaft itself, creating an area of slightly larger diameter than the rest of the shaft—is a component attachment system that is still used today.

Early on, archers experienced problems attaching outserts to carbon shafts in a perfectly aligned manner which, of course, adversely affected accuracy. But today manufacturers build outserts to exact tolerances, and the bugaboos of attaching them to the shaft have been reduced.

OUTSERTS AND FLETCHES

Besides the trouble with assembling the finished shaft, there are two other problems with building carbon arrows.

First, a broadhead outsert requires that the archer use a shaft an inch longer than the

arrow length would be if he or she were using the internal components as for aluminum arrows. Failure to do so results in a shaft that, when drawn, will see the outsert skip over, and sometimes off, the arrow rest. And second, the overhang from the outsert often catches on the batting of a target, making it difficult to pull the shaft out of the target.

Second, fletching has always been a problem for carbon arrows.

"In the early days, the available adhesives didn't work all that well when it came to securing fletching to the carbon shaft," concedes McNail. "We've tried many different things over the years, from sanding the bottoms of the vanes and the shaft to create a rough edge to trying all kinds of different glues and glue systems. Today, however, adhesion is not a real problem, as glue makers have developed some excellent adhesives for carbon shafts. For example, the Arizona Fast-Set Gel along with plastic vanes works extremely well on carbon shafts today."

Achieving adequate fletch clearance with the arrow rest has been one of the primary dilemmas with carbon shafts. Without adequate clearance, of course, bow tuning becomes problematic. Clearance glitches occur because with the extremely small diameter of carbon arrows, the fletching ends up being glued very close together on the shaft. Achieving perfect fletch clearance when using popular prong- or launcher-type arrow rests becomes more difficult than when using larger-diameter aluminum shafts, but with careful tuning you can avoid this problem.

The recent introduction of a "fatter" carbon arrow that accepts the same internal component systems used in aluminum arrows has solved the problems of fletch clearance and outserts. Two companies—Beman and Gold Tip—began using internal component systems in their pure carbon shafts in 1997. AFC/Game Tracker followed suit in 1998, with the Carbon

Smaller carbon shaft diameters may cause fletching clearance problems.

Impact Fat Shaft and Carbon Tech CT Rhino first appearing in 1999. These shafts accept the internal component systems because their finished shafts are a bit larger in diameter than the original carbon arrow.

"The larger-diameter carbon shafts are the wave of the future," McNail predicts. "They offer all the performance benefits of the smaller-diameter shafts but make achieving fletch clearance so much easier. That makes it easier to tune the bow properly with them, which of course leads to the ultimate in accurate shooting."

ABRASIVENESS

The last problem I'll mention regarding carbon shafts is carbon fiber's extreme abrasiveness. Shooting carbon shafts across the arrow rest leads to a high heat buildup, which rapidly destroys the rubber and/or plastic shrink tubing commonly used to help silence the sound of a shaft as it is drawn and shot across the metal prongs of a shoot-through rest.

As mentioned in chapter 2, I tried removing any form of silencing material from my rest prongs one season because I hadn't found a material that would withstand a couple hundred shots with carbon shafts. My pure carbon shafts actually wore grooves in the metal prongs of my shoot-through rest! To date, no arrow rest manufacturer has been able to completely solve this abrasion problem, although some companies are marketing Teflon launcher arms as a remedy. I use stick-on felt or moleskin, which will also wear out but is easy and inexpensive to replace.

PREFERRED CARBON ARROW FLETCHING & BROADHEADS

"The standard hunting fletch for carbon shafts is a 4-inch plastic vane," McNail notes, "although some hunters like 3 1/2-inch vanes when shooting mechanical heads." Generally speaking, when using poltruded shafts, you need either straight fletch or just 1 to 2 degrees offset, but when using a fatter shaft with an internal component system, you can get by with 2 to 3 degrees of offset to ensure fletch clearance with the arrow rest. This

Modern-day fatter shafts allow you to use inserts.

also can vary with the rest type. Some bowhunters prefer feathers to vanes, and they work well with carbon arrows too.

Shooting carbon arrows requires using smaller-diameter, lighter-weight broadheads than shooting aluminum shafts does.

"Generally speaking, broadhead weight should be no more than 125 grains with carbon arrows," McNail advises. "Most bowhunters choose heads in the 85- to 100-grain size." With replaceable-blade broadheads, most hunters favor a cutting diameter between 1 and 1 1/8 inches. Also, many carbon arrow shooters like mechanical broadheads, which match well thanks to their low profile and the fact that the raw arrow speed generated by the light carbon arrows helps mechanical broadheads work properly.

WHAT DO THEY COST?

When they first appeared, carbon arrows cost a lot more than comparable aluminum shafts. However, as more manufacturers begin to produce and sell carbon arrows and as the technology to manufacture them continues to improve, the price keeps falling. Today the price of carbon shafts closely competes with aluminum.

Carbon arrows have a lot going for them and are worth looking into. I've shot them almost exclusively for several seasons and have been mighty impressed. Does that mean the aluminum arrow is ancient history? Not on your life. It just means that a new player has come to town, one that offers a viable alternative to aluminum shafts. The wise bowhunter will weigh the pros and cons of each before deciding which to carry afield this season.

ROLL YOUR OWN

A small but growing group of archers choose to build their own arrow shafts. It's one of those things that gives them a deep satisfaction, knowing that they control all facets of their arrows' performance in the field. Those who build their own shafts often take the time to "crest" them, a term meaning to add a colorful custom paint job to the tail end of the shaft that tells the world to whom the arrows belong. It's archery's answer to fly tying and ammunition reloading.

You can obtain all the tools and parts you need for building your own aluminum arrow shafts from several sources. Mail-order houses like Cabela's, Bass Pro Shops and Bowhunter's Discount Warehouse have archery specialty catalogs that offer lots of supplies. Your local archery pro shop can help you order tools and parts too.

Here's what you need to get started: raw arrow shafts of the proper spine; arrow point inserts; arrow nock system (insert and nock); arrow fletches (either plastic vanes or natural feathers); fletching jig and clamp(s); nock alignment tool (optional but handy); cleaning solvent like Prep-Rite or lacquer thinner; heat source (if using hot-melt glue like Ferr-L-Tite); super glue; Fletch-Tite; and an arrow cutoff saw.

Building arrow shafts isn't exactly the same as building the atom bomb. However, both take patience, attention to detail and the right equipment.

See the appendix on page 171 for a list of arrow component manufacturers and resources.

Building an Arrow—Step by Step

1 Select the right shaft. Using an arrow shaft selection chart to show you the size shafts you need, order them either through your local pro shop or directly from the manufacturer.

2 Prepare the shafts. You must clean the shafts before you can work on them. Use a solvent designed specifically for this, like Prep-Rite or Acetone. This step ensures that all adhesives will stick as advertised, which is especially important when you get to the fletching.

3 Install the nock system. Assuming you're using a tunable nock system, to install, you simply press the insert into the shaft, bonding it with a small bit of hot-melt glue or super glue. Make sure to spread the glue around the insert to evenly distribute weight. Then simply pop the nock into the insert.

4 Prepare the fletching jig. Quality fletching jigs have shaft holder slots that custom-fit themselves around the shaft. You also must set the fletching jig for the number of fletchings for each arrow (usually three) and the amount of spacing between fletches. Jigs are available in single- and multi-arrow models.

5 Glue the fletch. Fletches are held by clamps designed for use with the fletching jig. After inserting a single fletch into the clamp so nothing protrudes but the base, run a solid line of adhesive along the fletch base. Take care not to overload the fletch.

6 Place the clamp in the jig. Most clamps attach to the fletching jig with magnets, making it simple to adjust the position until it's just so. Make sure the fletching fits flush to the shaft with no gaps. For good luck, I like to add a dab of adhesive to the forward tip of the fletch. When most fletches rip off a shaft, this is where it begins; the extra dab helps prevent tearing. Let the adhesive dry for 10 to 20 minutes.

7 Cut the shaft. You need a shaft cutoff saw for this. While some manual saws will work, why risk it? Invest in a good high-speed electric model. You can get one for about $100, but if you're serious about building arrows, you need one. Needless to say, take care to measure your shaft precisely before cutting. I like to cut my shafts 1/4 to 1/2 inch longer than I actually need to allow for changes in arrow rest styles or changes in bow models. A slightly longer arrow will not affect the shaft's flight.

8 Deburr the shaft. After cutting the shaft, take a few seconds to deburr the rough edge. You can buy small tools designed for this, but an inexpensive steel wool pad works just as well. Deburring ensures that the insert adhesive will stick properly to the shaft.

9 Install the arrow point inserts. Follow the same process as installing the nock adapter. Use either hot-melt glue or super glue.

Rolling your own arrow shafts isn't for everyone. It takes time and effort and something else—a little voice deep inside egging you on, encouraging you to become committed enough to archery and bowhunting to give it a try. To paraphrase an old advertisement, "Try it— you just might like it!"

LIGHT VS. HEAVY ARROWS

One of the most debated topics in archery pro shops and bowhunting camps everywhere is the subject of light vs. heavy arrows and which is best for bowhunting. It's a complicated subject and one that really has no definitive answer simply because not all bowhunters need the same levels of performance.

For example, a bowhunter who spends his or her entire career shooting 150-pound or less white-tail deer from a treestand at ranges of 30 yards or less does not need the same performance required to take on an 800-pound bull elk, 1,000-pound Alaskan brown bear or 1,200-pound bull moose. Open-country hunters on foot, like those who stalk the Western plains for pronghorn and mule deer—which may require a relatively long shot—have different performance needs than treestand deer hunters.

While there are many armchair arguments on the light vs. heavy arrow topic, the bottom line in terms of performance really is not debatable at all. The ballistics of an arrow in flight fall under the

domain of proven scientific principles of motion and energy. The debatable part involves determining the best arrow for a particular type of bowhunting.

Before delving into the topic, it is important to point out that each arrow shaft type—light or heavy—has advantages and disadvantages for the bowhunter. Understanding these assets and liabilities is the key to making a decision based on the facts as they apply to your specific bowhunting needs. Also, in the discussion of light vs. heavy below, we assume that all things besides arrow shaft weight—bow draw weight, shaft length and so on—are equal.

TRAJECTORY AND ARROW FLIGHT

All arrow shafts fly in a horribly arcing trajectory. That's why learning to estimate distance from the shooter to the target is the most important thing a bowhunter can master (after learning the fundamental mechanics of good bow shooting with a properly tuned bow-and-arrow setup).

The key advantage to a light shaft over a heavy one is that it leaves the bow at a higher velocity and thus has a flatter trajectory. This makes distance estimating a bit less critical at longer, unknown ranges. The heavier arrow follows a more arcing path, making estimating distance more critical and allowing less room for vertical aiming error.

REDUCING ARROW SHAFT WEIGHT

Most serious bowhunters try to increase arrow speed as much as they possibly can without sacrificing too much in the process. To do this, you can switch to lighter arrow shafts, shorten the overall arrow shaft length by attaching an overdraw to the bow, reduce the weight of the broadhead or field point, use lighter arrow fletching and broadhead inserts, increase the bow's draw weight... or a combination of all these techniques.

In one test, I shot four different arrow shaft types from one of my hunting bows, set at 78 pounds, through a chronograph. All were 30-inch arrows, all had 125-grain heads attached and all were properly spined for this bow. A heavy 2317 Easton aluminum shaft weighing 625 grains left the bow at 220 fps. A SuperLite Easton 2514 weighing 570 grains left the bow at 230 fps. A 525-grain AFC carbon shaft weighing 525 grains left the bow at 235 fps. And an Easton A/C/C aluminum-carbon composite shaft weighing 485 grains left the bow at 246 fps. By simply switching arrow shaft types and reducing the overall shaft weight, I can reduce arrow trajectory and give myself a bit more leeway when it comes to estimating distance to the target.

Despite many people's thinking, increasing the bow's draw weight is not the best way to achieve increased arrow speed. Most bow-and-arrow combinations tune best at a specific draw weight, and it's not always the same even for identical bows shooting identical arrows. For example, I own two completely indentical hunting bows. Using the same arrow shafts, one tunes perfectly at 74 pounds, while the other tunes best at 70 pounds. When the latter bow is cranked up to the 74-pound mark, the shafts begin to wobble slightly to the side, resulting in mediocre accuracy. Be that as it may, for every pound of draw weight added to your bow, arrow speed will increase approximately 1.75 fps.

Are the slight gains in trajectory, and therefore in margin of distance-estimating error, worthwhile? Hunting open country, where shots can be longer than 30 yards, any help you can get is worth it. At ranges under 30 yards, like with most treestand hunting situations, it really doesn't make enough difference to worry about.

LIGHT ARROWS: THERE'S NO FREE LUNCH

Before rushing out to purchase a barrel full of ultralight arrows, remember that, as with all good things in life, there is no free lunch. All good things have their price. When it comes to arrow shaft weight, you pay the price in kinetic energy.

First, all things being equal, a lighter arrow shaft always leaves the bow with less kinetic energy than a heavier shaft. Here are two examples.

A medium-weight, 30-inch Easton 2315 aluminum arrow weighs in at 545 grains and leaves a 60-pound bow at roughly 230 fps. That gives it a kinetic energy (KE) of 64.6 foot-pounds (fp). A relatively light 30-inch 2413 aluminum shaft weighs in at 446 grains and leaves the bow at 250 fps, with a KE of 62.9 fp. The lighter shaft has roughly 2.8 percent less energy than the heavier one. At the 40-yard line, the difference between the two has widened. The 2315 travels at 219 fps and carries a KE of 58 fp. The 2413 now travels at 234 fps, carrying a KE of 54.2 fp.

For this hunting situation, shaft weight is irrelevant. More important is whether or not you can place your arrow where you want it.

Arrow Shafts

An arrow shot at a big animal like an elk requires a lot of kinetic energy to penetrate cleanly and kill.

fletches used on fatter aluminum shafts.

If there were no arrow shaft in the bow at the time it was fired, the energy generated would be constant every shot (assuming the bow didn't blow apart when dry-fired). When you use arrow shafts of different weights, the KE transferred to the shafts differs, as we have seen. The question then becomes, where does the remaining energy go?

The energy vibrates through your bow's riser, limbs, cables, wheels and other attached parts. This vibration causes bow noise, which can spook animals at close range. Laboratory tests have shown that, all things being equal, the same bow shooting lighter arrows produces a higher amount of noise at the shot than when shooting heavier shafts.

This same vibration strains bow parts. Manufacturers have documented that bows shooting lighter shafts have a higher degree of failure in the handle, riser, limbs, cables and bowstring than those shooting heavier shafts. That's why AMO has developed a chart (see next page) based on extensive bow-handle tests, listing safe minimum arrow weights. The chart can also serve as a guideline for choosing minimum arrow weights for optimum performance.

That's the price you pay when you drop your arrow weight 100 grains without adding draw weight. From the time of shaft release to the 40-yard line, the heavier 2315 lost 6.2 percent of its initial velocity, while the lighter 2413 lost 8.2 percent. The lighter shaft also carries 6.8 percent less KE than the heavier shaft.

If you drop even more arrow shaft weight, as some speed-hungry bowhunters tend to do, you lose even more energy, especially at extended ranges. For example, if you drop from a 600-grain arrow to a 350-grain arrow, the difference in penetrating power between the two at the shot will be nearly 8 percent and will jump to nearly 20 percent at 40 yards.

OTHER PERFORMANCE VARIABLES

Other variables also affect performance. For example, the greater the drag on the shaft's rear end (caused by air resistance on the fletching), the quicker the lighter shaft will decelerate. That's a big reason to use 4-inch fletches for lightweight, small-diameter carbon and aluminum-carbon composite arrow shafts instead of the 5-inch

SHAFT WEIGHT AND PERFORMANCE ON GAME

When hunting deer-sized animals, the difference in kinetic energy between light and heavy arrow shafts is not worth worrying about. Assuming you are using high-quality broadheads with razor-sharp blades with either setup, on a broadside shot you'll more than likely shoot right through the animal.

However, on larger game like caribou, elk, moose and big bears, ultralight arrows might pose a problem in terms of getting the desired complete pass-through. The loss of 20 percent of downrange KE at 40 yards can result in a loss of penetration of a few inches. This could mean the difference between punching the broadhead through both sides of the hide—which results in more rapid blood loss and an easier tracking job—and puncturing only one side of the hide. It can mean the difference between punching a hole through one lung or both lungs. These are factors you should consider when deciding what type of setup to take on a hunt for these animals.

The objective, of course, is to make it as easy as possible for bowhunters to place their broadhead-tipped shaft into the vitals of the game animal they are hunting, hitting that animal with sufficient energy to take out both lungs and cause a rapid, humane death. When talking with many shooters at archery shops, on indoor shooting lanes and at 3-D shoots, I find that many of them get so wrapped up in the nuances of bow performance that they forget the objective of all of this. When setting up your bow for the coming season, have fun experimenting with different shaft sizes and weights, but remember that unless you can tune the bow-and-arrow combination with broadheads, then consistently hit your target, it won't matter how fast the bow shoots. You simply miss.

AMO Minimum Weight Chart

*Arrow Weight

Arrow weights are measured in grains and include allarrow components – shaft, insert, UNI bushing, point, fletching & nock.

**Stored Energy

Based on:
• 360 Grain Arrow
• 30" Draw Length
• 60" Peak Weight
• Speed (Hard) Cam

Abbreviations

S.E. = Stored Energy
E.S.E. = Energy Storage Efficiency
B.H. = Brace Height
P.D.F. = Peak Draw Force

Weight Conversions

1 ounce = 437.5 grains
1 gram = 15.4 grains

Actual Peak Bow Weight (lbs)				AMO Minimum Recommended Arrow Weights* (Grains)								
RECURVE	ROUND WHEEL	ENERGY WHEEL (Soft Cam)	SPEED CAM (Hard Cam)	Using the AMO Minimum Recommended Weight Chart: • Select the column that describes the type of bow you shoot. • Move down the column to the bow weight range that includes your Peak Bow Weight • Move horizontally across that row to your "AMO Draw Length" column. • The box at that location contains the recommended weight.								
S.E.** =.95 P.D.F.	S.E.** =1.04 P.D.F.	S.E.** =1.20 P.D.F.	S.E.** =1.3+ P.D.F.				• AMO DRAW LENGTH •					
E.S.E. 62 B.H. 9.5	E.S.E. 65.6 B.H. 9.0	E.S.E. 71.3 B.H. 8.0	E.S.E. 75.1 B.H. 7.0	25"	26"	27"	28"	29"	30"	31"	32"	33"
33	32	29	27	150	150	150	150	150	150	150	150	150
34-41	33-38	30-35	28-32	150	150	150	150	150	150	150	151	165
42-46	39-43	36-39	33-36	150	150	150	150	150	163	179	195	211
47-52	44-49	40-44	37-41	150	150	150	167	185	203	222	240	258
53-58	50-54	45-49	42-46	150	163	183	203	224	244	264	285	305
59-63	55-60	50-54	47-50	172	195	217	240	262	284	307	329	352
64-69	61-64	55-59	51-55	202	227	251	276	300	325	350	374	399
70-75	65-71	60-64	56-60	232	259	286	312	339	365	392	419	445
76-81	72-76	65-70	61-65	262	291	320	348	377	406	435	463	492
82-86	77-81	71-74	66-69	292	323	354	385	416	446	477	508	539
87-92	82-87	75-79	70-74	322	355	388	421	454	487	520	553	586
93-99	88-94	80-85	75-80	352	387	422	457	492	532	581	629	676

Arrow Shafts

Chapter 5

BROADHEADS FOR BOWHUNTING

One bright sunny afternoon, as I was walking down an old Missouri riverbottom after a week of heavy rain, heading for a treestand I'd set that morning, I accidentally stumbled over a dirt clod. Looking down, something caught my eye, so I picked it up. It was a perfectly shaped flint arrowhead, the kind that the first bowhunters made for hunting small game and birds. Next to it was a larger arrowhead, thick at the base but tapered to a sharp edge. This one was more suitable for killing deer, or even people.

I took a few minutes to wash these ancient arrow points in the creek, then sat on a stump and thought about them. I wondered what the ancient craftsman was thinking as he carefully knapped these heads. Did he thrill to the hunt as I do now, or was his work a more menial thing, part of the necessity for survival and nothing more? When he broke or lost one of his arrowheads, did he mourn it, knowing full well the time and effort it would take to knap another?

Fortunately, modern bowhunters have it much easier. Today it's simple to obtain a half-dozen space-age broadheads with blades so sharp they scare you. Modern broadhead design is evolving at a rapid rate. Old-style broadheads with fixed, resharpenable blades are giving way to both replaceable-blade and mechanical designs that are smaller, lighter and stronger.

But just because finding top-notch broadheads is a cinch, modern bowhunters should not lose sight of the fact that the purpose of the broadhead has not changed since the days when people knapped arrowheads from stone. The broadhead must fly straight and true, hold together upon impact, slice cleanly through flesh and blood and hold together and continue to do its job should it strike some bone.

Every time I attach a new broadhead to an arrow shaft, I can't help but think about the first bowhunters. Such reflection helps me appreciate how good I have it today. When you assemble the business end of your arrow shafts, can you feel their spirit within you? I can.

HOW DO BROADHEADS KILL GAME?

My mind was wandering the other day as I sat at my desk, doing my income taxes and wishing I were anywhere else.

On this particular day, I was thinking about a very large whitetail buck that walked near my stand in northeastern Kansas one cold November day. He came up out of a bottom and surprised me right at dark, and even though he came within 12 yards of my tree, I couldn't get on him. So I watched him walk over the hill and out of my life. But in my fantasy, he stopped broadside, and I drew my bow unseen and made the perfect release. I was so into my dream that I actually felt the broadhead strike him and pass clean through his chest.

That's when I jerked my hand up, shook my finger and watched blood ooze from a nasty slice near the tip. Instead of feeling the broadhead hit that buck, I had felt a nasty paper cut from an envelope full of W-2s. The paper's edge had made a neat, clean slice into the tip of my middle finger, and it took forever for the bleeding to stop.

BLOOD CLOTTING: HOW IT WORKS

Clean, neat cuts bleed and bleed and bleed and are as difficult to stop as a politician breaking a campaign promise. Conversely, an irregular wound that has been ripped or torn open clots relatively quickly, plugging itself up with jellied blood.

Why is this important to bowhunters? Our broadhead-tipped arrow shafts do their business best by causing massive blood loss. A smooth, razor-sharp broadhead that slices cleanly through game actually destroys relatively few body cells, creating minimal blood clotting and rapid blood loss. Conversely, a dull, ragged-edged broadhead damages a relatively high number of cells, which creates a more rapid clotting process.

Of course, broadheads can do other damage as well. A broadhead-tipped arrow that passes through an animal's boiler room can cause the lungs to collapse, the heart to stop and the liver and kidneys to cease functioning. This too will cause death. Razor-sharp blades will best get the broadhead to these vital organs, then all the way through them.

In short, a smooth-edged, razor-sharp broadhead is more conducive to rapid blood loss, which will result in a quick, humane death and an easier-to-follow blood trail than a broadhead with dull, ragged edges. To go afield with anything less than broadheads so sharp they scare you is both foolish and unethical.

GETTING THAT BROADHEAD THERE

What is the best broadhead to use? A wise-guy answer might be, "a sharp one." But the truth doesn't tell the whole story. A broadhead will do you absolutely no good if it does not fly accurately from your bow-and-arrow setup. After all, you render the world's most expensive broadhead useless if you can't hit the animal in the boiler room.

To fly like a dart, your broadhead must also be perfectly straight. If you've never given this a second thought, you should now.

On occasion, I've opened 3- and 6-packs of broadheads from several major manufacturers and found one or two of them out of alignment right from the get-go. With most reputable manufacturers today, this rarely, if ever, occurs. But I promise you it will happen to you if you shoot cheap broadheads long enough.

Also, broadheads that have been shot into targets frequently, or into a game animal, may end up with a bent ferrule. This bend usually occurs where the threaded ferrule meets the solid blade base, right where the head screws down tightly onto the arrow shaft insert.

To see whether your broadheads are bent, give them the spin test. Screw them into an arrow shaft you know is straight, then spin the broadhead like a top on its tip. If you see any wobble—look closely where the ferrule meets the shaft insert—

Today's broadheads are razor sharp right out of the box.

Always Use a Broadhead Wrench!

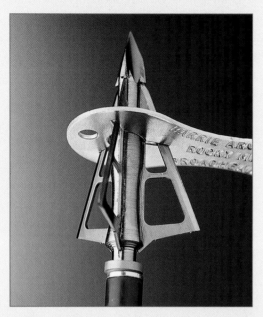

When putting fixed- and replaceable-blade broadheads on arrow shafts and removing them, always use a broadhead wrench. This tool, which comes free with virtually every pack of broadheads sold, will protect your fingers and hands from those razor-sharp blades.

It is easy to get in a hurry and not use the wrench, or, after time, to become so jaded that you figure what the heck, I don't need a stupid broadhead wrench, those things are for sissies. Then before you know it, you're bleeding all over yourself after the broadhead you were screwing onto your shaft slipped in your sweaty fingers. I have a friend who missed a week of bowhunting during the whitetail rut after cutting himself this way and visiting the emergency room to recieve more stitches than he cared to count.

Be smart. Play it safe. Keep a broadhead wrench in your tackle box, in your daypack and on your workbench, and always use it. That way you'll never have to say you're sorry ... or miss your target.

something is crooked. Since you already checked the arrow shaft for straightness, you know it's the broadhead. When this happens to me, I try the head on a different shaft just to be sure, but I can generally predict the results—more wobble.

Don't even think about trying to straighten out that broadhead: Throw it away. It may have cost five bucks, and it hurts to throw a Lincoln into the garbage, but it will hurt even more should you try to hunt with that head and miss (or worse yet wound and lose) the biggest buck of your life because you were too cheap to buy another 3-pack of broadheads.

One other point. To ensure that your broadheads fly like darts, you must both tune your bow with broadheads and shoot them before hunting. We'll talk more about bow tuning in Chapter 6, "Bow-Tuning Basics," and broadhead accuracy in Chapter 7, "How to Shoot Your Bow." Only a careless bowhunter skips these steps in the process.

Scalpel-sharp blades and a perfectly straight broadhead—the two will add up to bad news for the game in your area this season.

Check for flaws where the ferrule meets the shaft insert.

TYPES OF BROADHEADS

FIXED-BLADE BROADHEADS

Not long ago, bowhunters shot what were, by today's standards, large and heavy broadheads that impeded arrow speed. These traditional-style, fixed-blade heads had a lot going for them, though. Of one-piece construction featuring a flat main blade generally made from welded steel, they were incredibly strong. Their cut-to-tip design fostered deep penetration. The combination of heavy head weight and relatively heavy arrow shafts with their bullet-proof construction and razor-sharp edges helped them penetrate deeply and crack even the heaviest rib bones.

Despite the availability of high-quality replaceable-blade broadheads of a more modern design, many bowhunters still choose to use traditional heads that need to have an edge put on them. Readily available examples include many old favorites—like the Zwickey Black Diamond and Black Diamond Eskimo, Bear Razorhead, Delta Rothhaar Snuffer and Nubbin, and Magnus and Magnus II—as well as modern versions including the Simmons Landshark 125, Landshark 160 and Interceptor 190; Wolverine 130 and 160; Grizzly 100, 125, 145 and 160; and Patriot 105, 125 and 140. These two-bladed broadheads may or may not have small bleeder blades that have sometimes been presharpened at the factory.

Traditional broadheads attach in one of two ways to the arrow shaft. In the early years, all broadheads were glued onto the shaft. Many

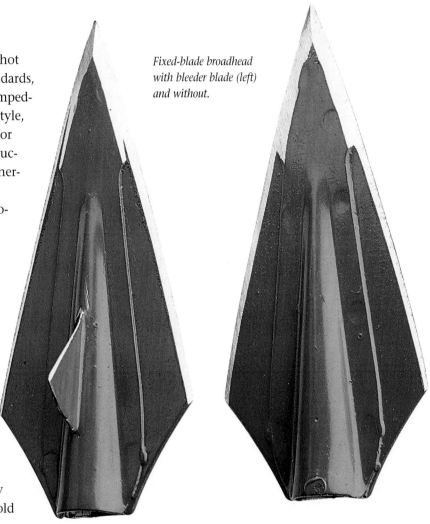

Fixed-blade broadhead with bleeder blade (left) and without.

archers who still use traditional broadheads prefer to glue them. This saves the extra weight added by a screw-in insert and forms a superb bond to the shaft. However, most modern-day bowhunters who choose traditional-style broadheads use a screw-in insert for convenience.

Traditional-style broadheads have their downside, of course. First, their heavy weight doesn't match up well with today's fast bows and lightweight arrow shafts. Some companies, like Patriot, have responded to that issue by offering heads weighing as little as 110 grains. Second, their flat blade design tends to bend slightly at

Broadheads for Bowhunting

Sharpening Traditional Broadheads

Sharpening traditional broadhead designs is an art lost to many contemporary bowhunters. If you're just starting out with these kinds of broadheads, it will help to find someone who has developed the skills needed to put the razor's edge on their own broadheads.

With main blades that have no edge on them at all, you can start with an 8-inch flat file to establish cutting bevels. Some people make a custom handle to hold the head when sharpening it; others sharpen it while it's on the arrow shaft. Either way you must be very careful not to slip and cut yourself. You might want to wear a pair of leather gloves as insurance against slippage and slight nicks. Once you have established cutting bevels, use an Arkansas whetstone to help refine the edge. Lastly, strop the head on a leather strop to help smooth the cutting edge to razor sharpness.

During this process, creating a bevel angle of between 30 and 36 degrees is about right. While some skilled bowhunters can maintain a consistent angle during the sharpening process, most of us can't. Using a commercially made sharpening tool or homemade jig will maintain an identical sharpening angle stroke after stroke. Keeping a consistent bevel angle is critical to achieving a shaving-sharp edge. Every time you roll the blade over and off the desired angle during the sharpening process, you slightly dull the blade and come closer to square one than a finished head. That's why some people never can seem to get a razor's edge on their blades. Using the commercial sharpening tools will help greatly.

the tip. These broadheads gain their strength from their blade thickness, often a minimum of .040 inch. And third, traditional broadhead edges require hand-sharpening, an art lost on many New Age archers.

But not all bowhunters have forgotten about these ageless broadheads. My friend Chuck Jones, host of a popular cable television hunting show and a professional videographer who currently films and hunts for the Knight & Hale Game Calls team, is also one of the finest whitetail bowhunters I've ever met. Chuck eschews modern technology in favor of traditional broadheads like the Simmons Landshark.

"When you hit a deer with one of these big, heavy heads, it's like hitting him with a chopping ax!" Jones says. The wound channel made by these large broadheads is something to behold, and should the shot be pulled a bit and the broadhead strike the shoulder blade, it will probably crack a hole right through the bone and still reach the lungs. And as Chuck says, when your shots are as close as they are for most treestand deer hunters, a little less arrow speed and a bit of trajectory loss should not make a difference. It is only when shot distances open up that this plays a role in the ability to hit the target.

While I personally rarely use this style of broadhead anymore, I have used it with deadly efficiency on game ranging from deer to bears to elk. The largest bull elk I've taken with a bow fell to a heavy Easton 2317 aluminum shaft and Delta Nubbin.

These timeless broadheads still have a lot to offer the modern bowhunter.

Broadheads come in different sizes with designs that continue to evolve and improve.

Their convenience and razor-sharp blades make replaceable-blade broadheads the tackle of choice these days.

REPLACEABLE-BLADE BROADHEADS

We all collect knickknacks and bric-a-brac that represent our loves in life. Hunters have antlers on the wall, art depicting wildlife and hunting scenes, and small bits of memorabilia associated with our days afield scattered about homes, workshops, garages and offices.

On top of my television set sits a very small collection of ancient broadheads crafted from obsidian and flint by hunters who had much more at stake when it came to sneaking within arrow range of a bird or mammal than we do today. I've stumbled across them from time to time as I have traveled the country to hunt big game with my modern archery tackle, and each time I find one it sends me daydreaming about those who came before us. Upon reflection, one can see that broadheads really have not changed all that much through the years. For example, you can find three-bladed broadheads made from metal that date back some 3,000 years to the Bronze Age. A design very similar to the Trocar tip popularized by Muzzy was built in the 14th century to penetrate the chain mail soldiers wore.

Today, broadhead designs are evolving more quickly than ever before. Old-style broadheads with fixed, resharpenable blades have, in large measure, given way to smaller, lighter replaceable-blade designs. In this world of metamorphosis, bowhunters should not forget the fact that the broadhead's purpose has not changed since the days when people knapped their own arrowheads from stone. It must fly straight and true, hold together upon impact and slice cleanly through flesh and blood. Ideally, it also holds together and continues to do its job if it strikes some bone. The better heads can withstand more. After all, who wants to spend five bucks on a broadhead that is ruined when it smacks the ground after a miss?

Manufacturers build modern replaceable-blade broadheads from a modular design. Instead of the single, welded blade of fixed-blade heads, replaceable-blade broadheads feature a single central ferrule, replaceable blades that lock into that ferrule, and a tip that may or may not be an integral part of the ferrule. (Some tips screw into the ferrule.) A ring at the rear of the ferrule locks the blades in place, when you screw the ferrule down into the arrow shaft's insert. There might be rubber O-ring between the locking ring and shaft insert.

You can select a replaceable-blade broadhead that's sized to handle the game you'll be hunting.

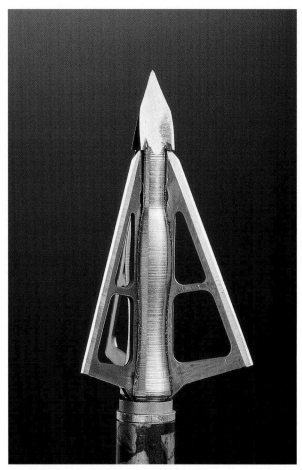

Barrie Archery's Ti 100 uses a titanium ferrule for maximum strength.

Smaller, Lighter Broadheads Are the Trend

Today's replaceable-blade broadheads, the product of a continuing evolution, have become smaller, lighter and manufactured to better tolerances than ever before.

"Lighter and smaller has become the industry trend with replaceable-blade heads over the past 10 years in terms of the product mix being sold," says Bob Mizek of New Archery Products, makers of the best-selling Thunderhead replaceable-blade broadhead line. "In the late 1980s and early 1990s, 145- and 125-grain broadheads were the big sellers," he comments. "We came out with our first 100-grain about a decade ago, and today it and our 125-grain are our biggest sellers. The lighter broadhead market—heads weighing 75 to 90 grains—is coming on too. I'd say it comprises about 20 percent of the market."

Dick Maleski of Wasp Archery Products notes, "In terms of weight, the most popular in the Wasp broadhead line are 100- and 125-grain, and then a large drop until the 75- and 85-grain class." Maleski, a pioneer in broadhead design, introduced his first replaceable-blade Wasp broadheads in the early 1970s.

"I think you'll see that the cutting diameter of replaceable-blade broadheads will stabilize at about 1 to $1^1/8$ inches as the most popular size overall, at least in the near future," predicts Bruce Barrie of Barrie Archery, makers of the superb Rocky Mountain broadhead line. "It used to be that the $1^1/2$- to $1^1/4$-inch cut was what people wanted, but now most people want the 1- to $1^1/8$-inch diameter. A lot of this is the result of the smaller-diameter, lighter arrows we're shooting today. These shafts have smaller vanes to steer them, and it is hard for them to steer the shaft properly when there is a large-diameter head on the shaft's nose. Also, the shorter, smaller-diameter, lighter-weight heads help achieve the proper weight-forward balance needed for dart-like arrow flight."

The most popular style of replaceable blade broadhead today is the three-blade design. "It's a three-blade game today," says Mizek. "I'd have to say 75 percent of the market is in three-blade heads." Chisel-type points sell better than any other type of three-blade heads. Second in popularity, the four-blade design features a cutting-tip design, Mizek describes.

Blade Sharpness

These days you have no excuse for hunting with dull broadheads. The increased popularity of replaceable-blade broadheads—the most popular broadhead style in the country today—has made using fresh, sharp blades as simple as tying your shoes.

"Since day one, serious bowhunters have appreciated the value of super-sharp blades," relates Andy Simo, president of New Archery Products. "Before I began making broadheads, I'd spend hours sharpening my heads until they were shaving sharp. These old carbon-steel blades rusted easily and quickly lost their sharpness. The frustration I felt led me to search for improved sharpening methods and materials."

"Anyone old enough to remember going to the

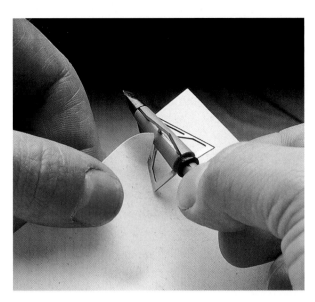

Test a broadhead's sharpness on paper.

barber shop for a shave remembers the leather strop hanging from the barber chair," Simo continues. "The strop would remove the jagged edge and fine burrs left from sharpening. I figured that the same process could be used on broadheads." In the early 1980s, New Archery Products' Razorbak became the first mass-produced replaceable-blade broadhead to have ground, honed and stropped blades, with continual improvements made to the process over the years until sharpness approached that of a surgeon's scalpel.

"There are several possible steps in the blade-sharpening process that a broadhead manufacturer can use," explains John Musacchia Jr. of Muzzy Products. "These include lapping, honing, stropping and polishing. The best and sharpest broadheads out there strop and polish their blades, which helps them achieve scalpel-like sharpness. That's our goal with Muzzys."

Even with this kind of commitment to quality, bowhunters should check each and every blade before heading into the woods.

"In a mass-produced product like broadheads and broadhead blades, there will be some variations in sharpness from blade to blade," explains Bruce Barrie. "If we made them one blade at a time, we could polish each and every blade to perfection. But it's not economically feasible for us or any other broadhead maker that does a large business volume. I'd say that, by and large, 98 percent

Tip Design & Penetration

There are three basic tip designs on modern replaceable-blade broadheads—cutting tip, chisel point and conical point. Which is best for bowhunting?

In the old days, when arrow speeds of 200 fps were hot and arrow shafts were as heavy as logs, the cutting-tip design first found on fixed-blade broadheads was the best choice. Still found on several modern replaceable-blade broadheads—designed to be shot from bows producing modern arrow speeds of up to 300 fps—cutting-tip broadheads remain an excellent choice.

However, the chisel-point design is just as good in terms of penetration and perhaps a bit better in terms of overall strength and durability. Chisel-point tips feature flattened surfaces that are beveled to a sharp tip. Many broadhead makers today add a small hollow grind to their chisel tips, reducing friction on impact. They also sharpen the edges—and many bowhunters hand-sharpen the edges of those that do not come presharpened. Recent tests have shown that well-made chisel-point broadheads from top manufacturers penetrate just as deeply as heads of the cutting-tip design.

Conical-tip broadheads are beginning to fade from the scene, being

(From left) Cutting tip, conical tip, chisel tip.

replaced by chisel-point tips. The smooth, rounded surface of the conical tip tends to slide along the hide of an animal upon impact on all but broadside shots, impeding penetration.

of the replaceable blades that either come with a package of broadheads or in separate blade replacement packs should be sharp enough to hunt with. Bowhunters should certainly check them out, either by trying to shave arm hair or by cutting a single sheet of medium-weight typing paper. If they'll do either of these things, you're okay."

"If the blade isn't sharp enough, throw it away and insert a fresh blade. That's the whole point of replaceable blades—to throw it out and use a fresh blade when the first is too dull to hunt with," adds Barrie. "That dullness might come from the factory, or it might come from target practice. Whatever the reason, you want to be hunting with nothing but sharp, sharp blades."

MECHANICAL BROADHEADS

Remember riding around in the car with your parents, driving them crazy putting your flattened hand out the window and making it go up, down and all around by simply changing the position of your fingers? Little did you know that this torment was really a demonstration in aerodynamics, showing that as the position of the hand changed, so did the aerodynamic loading, which in turn pushed or pulled the hand in a specific direction.

The same test is performed every time you shoot a broadhead-tipped arrow. The broadhead blades act as airfoils that, unless everything is perfectly aligned and symmetrical and adequately

Care of Sharpened Broadheads

The treatment of sharpened broadheads is just as important as putting a razor's edge on the blades. It makes no sense to create or purchase shaving-sharp broadheads only to let them become dull in storage or in your quiver.

Excellent commercially made broadhead boxes—from MTM Products, Bohning and others—hold sharpened heads in either a Styrofoam block protected by a sturdy plastic box or in small plastic boxes that hold each head individually to keep them from banging together. Most quivers also have Styrofoam broadhead holders, while some feature individual compartments designed to hold single heads firmly and apart from others.

Some bowhunters like to either coat their broadheads lightly with mineral oil or, like me, spray them with a light machine oil like Rem-Oil, WD-40 or similar product. In the old days of carbon-steel blades, coating broadheads with mineral oil, then wrapping them individually with a piece of paper towel, helped prevent both dulling and rust.

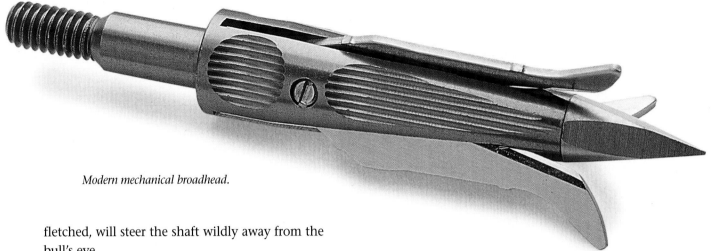

Modern mechanical broadhead.

fletched, will steer the shaft wildly away from the bull's eye.

This tendency is the big reason mechanical, or expandable, broadheads have become increasingly popular in recent years. Their development goes hand in hand with the proliferation of today's super high-speed bows and lightweight arrow shafts with small fletching, a combination more difficult to tune precisely with the large-diameter, fixed- and replaceable-blade broadheads that have been a mainstay of bowhunting since its earliest days.

Mechanical Heads: What Are They?

A mechanical broadhead features blades—usually two or three—connected to the ferrule by a hinge system, which allows them to be folded into the ferrule before the shot. Upon contact with an animal, the blades drive outward until they lock into the ferrule. Now in the same cutting position as blades found on fixed-blade broadheads, mechanical broadhead blades will perform the same cutting function.

The advantages of this system are many. First, by removing the airfoil of the fixed blades and creating a low-profile arrow tip, expandable-blade broadhead-tipped arrows fly almost identically to arrows with target tips of the same weight. The superior aerodynamics of these heads were designed to be used with high-speed compound bows pushing small-diameter, lightweight arrow shafts—specifically carbon and aluminum-carbon composite arrows—with small fletching at 250 fps or more.

Their low profile also makes a bow-arrow-broadhead combination a bit easier to tune precisely than when using fixed-blade broadheads. And expandable broadheads achieve a wider cutting path through an animal than most popular fixed-blade heads of the same weight. While the most popular fixed-blade broadheads have a cutting diameter of between 1 and $1^1/4$ inches, most expandables start at $1^1/4$ inches, with most in the $1^7/8$- to $2^1/2$-inch range. In bowhunting, the bigger the hole, the better.

Mechanical Broadhead Construction

In their brief history, mechanical broadheads have experienced a jump from cheap materials and poor construction to the use of the best materials and construction out there, at least from the better manufacturers.

For example, the Spitfire line from New Archery Products features top-of-the-line 6262 T-9 aircraft aluminum ferrules, the same material used in their popular Thunderhead replaceable-blade broadhead line for many years. Many other makers also use high-grade aircraft aluminum for their ferrules, including 6061 T6.

The best mechanical heads use blades made from the same materials found on top replaceable-blade heads too. That means high-grade stainless steel with a high carbon and chromium content, which translates into sharpness and durability.

This includes both 440C steel—which top knife makers use for their blades—and 420C stainless steel. New Archery Products has gone so far as to give their blades a "diamize" finish.

"This is our own trademarked process," says Bob Mizek of New Archery Products. "What it does is put a super-fine finish across the whole cutting surface on the blade where the grinding has occurred. By doing this, there is less heat buildup during the grind, and you don't get any annealing of the blade edge. This is a 'gentle' final grinding process that results in a super-fine edge and, more importantly, a more durable edge. We do this now on all our blades, including our Thunderheads."

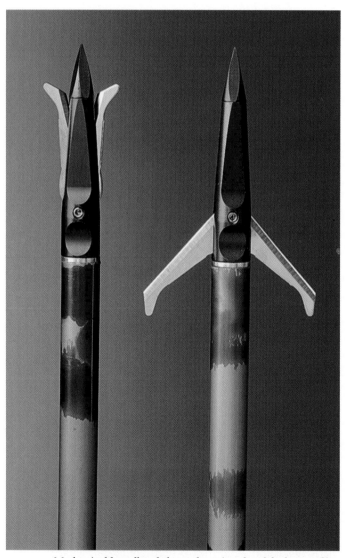

Mechanical broadheads leave the string closed for low-profile flight (left) and expand upon impact for maximum cutting diameter (right).

The Trade-Offs

As with all things in life, everything involves a trade-off. And expandable-blade broadheads are no exception.

While great strides have been made in this regard, it still takes more kinetic energy than it does with traditional and replaceable-blade broadheads to ensure that the blades on these new broadheads will open as designed and still perform their cutting and penetrating functions.

Also, with the product still in its infancy, basic design and construction continues to evolve. Some expandables are poorly constructed with thin blades and poor manufacturing tolerances, creating a product that may work on thin-skinned deer-sized game under perfect conditions but may not perform well on angled shots or larger animals.

Finally, though no empirical research has been done on this topic, serious shooters are debating the subject of "arrow whip" when discussing expandables. Arrow whip means that on an angled shot, the first blade to strike the animal will open before the others, causing the shaft to whip out to the side. This would redirect much of the shaft's kinetic energy and seriously impede penetration. Because of these questions, several big-game guides have told me they will not allow mechanical broadheads to be used in their camps.

Also, many lazy bowhunters are switching to expandable broadheads for the wrong reasons, using their relatively easy tunability as a crutch for less-than-meticulous bow tuning and sloppy shooting form. Jim Dougherty—one of the pioneers of bowhunting, a former pro shop owner, and currently a spokesman for Easton arrow shafts—has this to say: "Any broadhead, if the component parts are straight and it is concentrically mounted on the correct arrow shaft with proper fletching, will shoot well. This includes the old-style, fixed-blade heads. Today there's an infusion of 'gimmick' models arriving on the scene, and I think it's an irresponsible approach, motivated purely by profit and attended by hype."

Dougherty says—and I concur—that regardless of the broadhead style one chooses to shoot, great care must be taken to tune the bow-arrow-broadhead combination properly. The shooter must also practice enough that his or her shooting form and skills are honed to the same fine edge that his broadhead blades are before heading afield.

Mechanical Broadhead Trends

Who uses the mechanical broadhead today? According to industry representatives, the typical bowhunter switching to mechanical heads has recently switched from a mid-performance-level bow that sends arrows downrange in the 220 to 240 fps range to a high-speed bow that propels arrows in the 250 to 290 fps range. Suddenly, this hunter finds that the new bow may be a bit fussier to set up and tune than the old bow and that it's more critical of slight errors in shooter form. Thus, the hunter must reevaluate available arrow tips to be able to translate all this new high performance into accuracy.

The trend is also moving away from two-blade heads and toward three-blade heads. With reduced KE requirements for optimum performance, it just makes sense to use a broadhead that provides more overall cutting surface.

"In general, the industry realizes now that the oversized cutting hole isn't all that critical," Mizek admits. "The trend I see is manufacturers moving away from broadheads that produce cutting holes over 2 inches in diameter and instead moving into something more like $1^1/_2$ inches. This gives the broadhead a lot more durability and penetration while still producing a hole that's plenty big enough to get the job done."

My limited personal experience with expandables extends more to the testing grounds than to the field. I have hunted with expandables, taking a handful of whitetail deer and a large Alaskan black bear, all of which went less than 40 yards after being hit. While I've found that most expandables tune well and fly like darts, I've never had a problem tuning my bows to shoot just as well with just as much velocity with well-made replaceable-blade heads. The large-diameter exit hole created by the expandable's ultrawide cutting surface is awesome to say the least, and is a definite advantage.

My feelings remain mixed. Keep in mind that mechanical broadheads are not legal in all states at this time. While expandable heads may be the wave of the future and are worth checking out, do so carefully before making the switch. Go to your local archery pro shop and ask their experts for help in selecting an expandable to try out. And remember the words of Jim Dougherty—"When it comes to broadheads, I want no toys, no gimmicks. Just clean-cutting points, hard steel and sharp edges."

Target & Field Points

*I*n addition to broadheads, you'll need both target points and field points to complete your setup.

For basic target shooting into soft targets—like hay bales, Styrofoam, compressed cardboard and life-sized 3-D animal targets—you need target points, those bullet-shaped arrow tips that penetrate easily into, and are easily pulled out of, your targets. They come in a wide variety of weights—from 65 grains all the way up to 180 grains—and diameters—which include $^{20}/_{64}$, $^{21}/_{64}$ and $^{22}/_{64}$ inch.

Choose a target tip that matches shaft diameter to achieve the optimum in aerodynamics, as well as to make it easy to pull shafts from the target. Also, be sure to match the weight of your target tip to the broadheads you plan on shooting. It makes no sense to tune your bow to shoot 125-grain target tips if you plan to bowhunt with 100-grain broadheads.

Choose a target tip matched to your regular broadhead weight.

Most target and field points screw into standard arrow shaft inserts. However, at least one company, Game Tracker/AFC, sells glue-in target points for carbon arrows. These points are designed to slide down into the shaft, eliminating the need for an outsert that would make it very difficult to pull these small-diameter arrows from targets. Of course, these shafts will not be good for bowhunting, but if you hunt with pure carbon arrows that require a broadhead outsert, it may be worthwhile to set up a half-dozen or so shafts with these glue-in practice points for nothing more than target shooting.

Field Points

Field points—arrow points designed to permit easy in-the-field practice like stump shooting—come in a wide variety of shapes, styles and weights, and again screw into a standard arrow shaft insert.

My all-time favorite arrow points for both stump shooting and hunting small game like rabbits and squirrels are the Zwickey Judo Point and Game Tracker/AFC Shocker. These feature a weighted tip, with the Judo having four small spring arms set 90 degrees from each other and the Shocker bearing five small spring arms set 72 degrees from each other. The spring arms prevent the arrow from skipping a million miles after you've shot it into grass or dirt, making arrow recovery a lot easier than when using a smooth point of some sort. The springy arms also open a large wound channel in small game or birds, ensuring a quick, humane death without destroying a lot of meat. Judos are available in 100-, 125- and 135-grain weights, Shockers in 100- and 125-grain sizes. Other tips of this type include the Satellite Grabber, in 100- and 125-grain sizes, and the Condor Judo Point, which weighs 105 grains and has springy arms that span 2¹/₈ inches.

You can also find a variety of blunt-type field points available as well. My favorite for both in-the-field practice and small-game hunting is the Saunders Bludgeon. Screw-in Bludgeons come in 85-, 125- and 145-grain weights and feature a hard, rubbery plastic head with several small, tapered rub-

Bludgeon point.

ber points on the end. They really smack small game and are excellent for field practice too. Other rubber blunt tips—like the HTM Small Game Blunt, designed to slip over your target point or the end of your arrow shaft—also work well for this.

Judo point.

SMALL GAME POINTS

For serious small-game hunting, the Adder Point is something else. The Adder is a metal ring that closely matches the diameter of the end of your arrow shaft and has eight small, wicked cutting edges coming off it, like a tiny star. To use one, simply place it between the arrow shaft and a standard field point, then screw the field point down tight. It's excellent for small game or turkeys.

Grasshopper.

Field point.

Often used with a field point for small-game hunting or behind a broadhead when turkey hunting to impede penetration and hopefully prevent a pass-through, the Muzzy Grasshopper and Zwickey Scorpio are small metal circles that fit between either a field tip or broadhead and feature four small spring arms similar to those found on Judo or Shocker points. They work very well.

Another field tip type is the Snaro Bird Point. Designed for hunting birds in flight, they're also used for rabbits, squirrels and small game birds on the ground. They feature a metal tip and four small wire loops in two sizes—three-inch diameter and six-inch diameter. Also available are square-cut metal field points, called metal blunts.

Field Point Maintenance

Field points require little mainte-nance. However, I do a couple of things to ensure that my arrows contin-ue to fly straight and true with field points attached.

Before screwing these points into my arrows, I like to apply a small amount of light machine oil, like WD-40 or Rem-Oil, to the threads. This makes it easy to remove the field points once I'm done and also inhibits rust.

After a day of small-game hunting or stump shooting, I wash my small-game points in warm soapy water to remove mud, grass and other gunk, dry them thoroughly, then spray all metal parts with the light oil. If the springy arms of a Judo or Shocker point have been bent, I use a pair of needle-nose pliers to bend them back into shape.

I use a small clear-plastic fishing tackle box with individual trays to store my field points, labeling each tray with an indelible marker so I can keep different types and weights of field points separate.

Broadheads for Bowhunting

Chapter 6

BOW TUNING BASICS

You know the age-old saying, "You have to learn to walk before you can run?" That's a good way to look at the bow-tuning process.

Shooting a bow at targets should be fun. Bowhunting is even more fun. But neither will be any fun at all if your bow-and-arrow setup is not capable of putting your arrows where you want them. That's where bow tuning comes in.

Bow tuning—the process of adjusting the various components that comprise your bow-and-arrow setup until they all work in concert, producing dart-like arrow flight—is the grunt work of the sport. Like football's interior linemen, you don't hear much about tuning until something's wrong. It is an essential part of archery that cannot be overlooked or forgotten. You can't take shortcuts, scrimp on time and effort or fudge anything. Unless you perform the tuning meticulously, you won't be satisfied with the result.

To the uninitiated, bow tuning may seem like some mystical process involving a mumbo-jumbo language that only expert archers understand. But it doesn't have to be this way. Approach bow tuning as a fairly simple thing. If the arrow does this, you do that until everything comes out the way it should. Sure, sometimes it can be frustrating. So can putting together your kids' toys at Christmas. But the smiles on their faces when they first see them makes it all worthwhile. Your face will look the same when you get that new bow shooting arrows like laser beams.

Even if your local archery pro shop assists you in tuning your bow, a basic understanding of both the process and the reasons behind it will help make you a better bow shot and make it possible for you to fix minor problems should they occur in hunting camp.

Want to learn more? Then read on as I translate the foreign language of bow tuning into plain English for you.

WHAT IS BOW TUNING?

instead of flying like a dart, wobbled down the range like a toddler just learning to walk. He had a serious tuning problem.

WHY BOW TUNING?

A tuning problem? Isn't that something found in race cars or orchestras?

Tuning problems also exist in the world of modern archery. Simply stated, bow tuning describes the need for and method of adjusting the relevant parts of your bow-and-arrow setup so that they work together to produce excellent arrow flight.

Tuning a longbow is a simple proces—really nothing more complicated than choosing arrow shafts of the correct spine and length, setting the nock point and checking the bow's brace height. Tuning a recurve bow that is shot "off the shelf" is similarly simple. If you choose to add an arrow rest, you must also consider centershot and fletch clearance.

But a compound bow is something else. With its intricate system of wheels and cables that both increase raw arrow speed and reduce the holding weight, a compound bow involves many more parts than traditional bows that you must adjust to work in sync. Also, the parts of the compound bow have less tolerance for error in these adjustments than either a recurve or longbow.

The wheel-and-cable system of a compound bow provides faster arrow flight than that of traditional equipment. It also provides more consistent arrow flight, which in turn leads to greater accuracy at distance. An out-of-tune bow will shoot arrows that wobble and float downrange. Sometimes you can see this knuckleball-like flight with the naked eye. Often, though, the wobble is subtle and can be detected only by the paper-tuning process (described in detail later in this chapter) and by the ability of the bow to shoot broadhead-tipped arrows into consistently tight groups at a distance.

The budding bowhunter left the shop with a dozen new arrows and a brand-new compound bow adorned with the latest arrow rest, fiber-optic bow sight, peep sight, two-piece bow quiver and hydraulic stabilizer. He stepped to the line at the outdoor target range, nocked an arrow, clipped his release to the bowstring and came to full draw. His new equipment had him brimming with confidence, and when his first shot hit three feet to the left of the bull's eye, he was a bit perplexed. Nocking another arrow, he was even more flummoxed when the next shot hit a foot high and to the right.

At his request I stood behind him, closely watching his arrow's flight on the next shot, which hit a bit low and left. That one shot told me everything I needed to know. His shaft,

Why bow tuning? Because without a properly tuned bow-and-arrow, your chances of consistently accurate shooting are nil. And that means increased frustration, less fun, and—most important to bowhunters—low odds for success when a deer or other big-game animal comes within range and it's time to draw and shoot.

COMPOUND BOWS: NOT ALL ARE CREATED EQUAL

The longer you play with compound bows, the more you realize that they're not all equal. Some are just more difficult to set up and tune than others. Every now and then, you'll find one that just refuses to shoot arrows the way it should. I used to let this bug the heck out of me. Occasionally I have spent several days trying to get a specific bow to tune, with no success, even after trying different arrow shaft sizes, different point weights and a couple of different arrow rests.

Now I do it differently. As my friend Randy Ulmer—arguably the finest competitive 3-D shooter of the last decade and a superb bowhunter—told me one day, "When I find a bow like that, rather than mess with it, I send it back. There's no reason bow tuning should be that difficult."

Randy's right. Today's high-tech bows are, as a rule, quite easy to set up and tune. This is especially true for release-aid shooters, simply because shooting a release produces less paradox (see below) than shooting with fingers. When I find a bow that gives me fits, I take it to my local pro shop, where the resident expert and I both work it over. If that doesn't do the job, I return it to the manufacturer with a nice letter asking for a replacement.

One final note before moving into the hows of bow tuning: Take your time and be meticulous in the tuning process. Don't be satisfied with mediocrity. A well-tuned bow that shoots laser beams for arrows is the foundation upon which you'll build accurate shooting—and, therefore, consistent success in the field.

Archer's Paradox

AMO defines paradox as "the timely flexing of the arrow as it passes around the bow handle and rest." In plain English that means: When you release an arrow shaft, it does not leave the bowstring in a perfectly straight manner. Instead, it violently flexes and bends before finally straightening out downrange. The amount of flexing and the distance from the bow at which the arrow finally straightens itself out are directly related to shaft spine and how well you've tuned the bow. That's why you must choose an arrow shaft of the right spine for your bow's draw length, draw weight and your release style, then tune your bow to shoot that specific shaft.

High-speed photography shows that arrows flex side to side when released with fingers, the first big bend being away from the bow riser and arrow rest. When you use a release aid, arrows "porpoise" or flex up and down. That's why fingers shooters are best served choosing cushion-plunger-style arrow rests, which have no parts for the shaft or its fletching to strike during that first big bend. It is also why release shooters are best served with shoot-through-type (prong-type) rests, which have no parts above or below the shaft and its fletching.

SETTING UP YOUR BOW

In preparing your bow for shooting, first set it up with all the accessories you'll be using while hunting, including: an arrow rest, bow sight, peep sight, bow quiver, nocking point or string loop, string silencers and stabilizer. Remember that any change in accessories once the bow has been set up and tuned, as well as a change in how you release your arrows or how you grip the bow, requires rechecking the tune.

HOW TO GO ABOUT IT

1 **Set the bow's tiller.** *AMO defines tiller as "the amount that the top handle/limb junction-to-string dimension is different than the bottom handle/limb junction-to-string dimension." Simply put, that means measuring the distance between the bowstring and the point where the bow limb meets the riser on both the bottom and top*

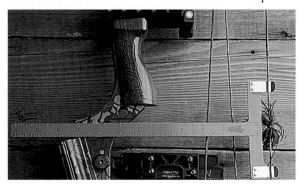

limbs. To begin with, these distances should be the same, which will help keep the wheels or cams in time with each other.

2 **Attach the arrow rest.** *Most modern arrow rests bolt onto the bow through a precut hole in the riser. A bow square will help you level the rest. Once you've secured the rest in place, set the centershot. AMO defines centershot as "the left/right horizontal placement of the arrow rest in the sight window of the handle riser." When using a release aid,*

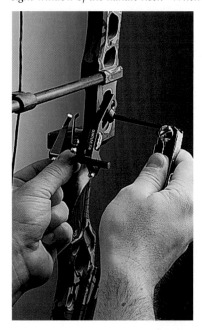

begin by setting the centershot dead on—that is, so that the arrow shaft is directly in line with the bowstring. If you shoot with fingers, it's best to start by setting the centershot a bit outside of center. You should barely be able to see the tip of the shaft to the left of the string (if you shoot right-handed). This helps compensate for archer's paradox.

3 **Attach the nock set or string loop.** *Using a bow square and nocking pliers, firmly attach a nock set to the string. It should be level with the arrow rest or slightly higher, no more than $1/4$ inch. If you will shoot a string loop, tie this on now instead of clamping on the nock*

set. Remember that you'll have to slide both up or down the string a bit during the tuning process, so don't clamp the ends on so tightly that you can't adjust them later.

4 **Attach the peep sight and string silencers.** Using a bow press, take the pressure off the bowstring until you can insert the peep sight between the bowstring strands. Take care to split the string evenly on both sides of the peep. To begin with, set the peep about 6 inches above the nock set. Use some waxed dental floss or extra bowstring material to tie a slip knot above and below the peep. You'll be able to slide the peep into the exact position later, then secure it with the slip knot. If your peep uses rubber tubing to help it come straight at full draw, attach it now. Now's the time to place your string silencers—Cat Whiskers, puff balls, Tarantulas or whatever—between the string strands, one each above and below the nock set. Place them equidistant from the bowstring serving and axle.

5 **Attach the bow sight.** Before bolting on a bow sight, I place some stick-on moleskin or felt between the riser and bow sight for padding, cutting holes to allow the bolts or screws easy access.

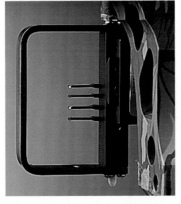

6 **Attach the bow quiver.** Again, use stick-on felt or moleskin to pad the riser before bolting on the quiver.

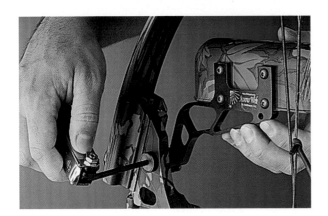

7 **Rotate the arrow nocks.** Assuming you have chosen the proper arrow shaft for your bow, have had it cut and fletched and have a target point of the proper weight installed, you can now rotate the arrow nocks to help minimize contact between the fletch and arrow rest during the shot. With a shoot-through rest and the use of a mechanical release aid, the cock vane should be straight down so it can pass easily between the rest prongs. With a cushion-plunger rest and fingers release, the cock vane should be rotated almost 90 degrees to the outside while eyeballing the two hen vanes to see that they are not going to hit the rest cushion.

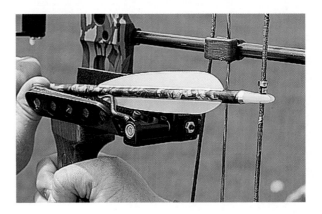

8 **Double-check everything.** Make sure to attach all your accessories securely to the bow. Double-check the tiller and nock height. Use a bow scale and note the draw weight. With no arrow on the string, come to full draw and check the position of the peep sight, adjusting it until you can see clearly through it while at full draw with your head erect (not hunched over) and the tip of your nose touching the bowstring.

Now take a deep breath and get ready. It's time to paper-tune the bow.

THE PAPER TUNING PROCESS

your setup to achieve top-notch arrow flight.

Much of the time, paper-tuning is a short process. If the bow and shaft are well matched, the accessories have been adjusted and attached to the bow properly and the arrow nocks rotated and eyeballed to avoid fletch contact with the rest, you will need to make few adjustments. But every now and then it takes a bit of time before everything works in concert.

THE IMPORTANCE OF FLETCH CLEARANCE

Your number-one concern is fletch clearance with the arrow rest and riser. You achieve the very best results when the shaft's fletching makes absolutely no contact with the arrow rest at all. However, minor contact usually takes place and is acceptable if it is indeed very minor.

During the initial tuning process, I spray a white foot powder, like Desenex or Micatin, on the fletching, rest and shaft, checking after each shot for disturbances in the powder residue that would indicate contact. You can usually eliminate contact by slightly rotating the arrow nock. Keep in mind, however, that you may never eliminate some slight contact. You might also want to check the arrow rest itself. You may have to bend some parts slightly out of the way or you might discover parts too thick or wide to permit clearance. Sometimes this means changing to a new rest. Regardless, be meticulous in your search for fletch clearance.

I have participated in few activities over the years that can, at times, frustrate me more, and yet can give me more pleasure, than paper-tuning a bow.

I cannot overemphasize the importance of the paper-tuning process. The reason is simple: Unless all the components of your bow-and-arrow setup work together in perfect harmony, you won't achieve good arrow flight. And without arrows that shoot downrange like little laser beams, consistent accuracy is impossible. Paper-tuning allows you to see what adjustments you need to make to

The Process

When paper-testing your shafts, it is very important that you take your time. Meticulous care in paper-testing that results in perfect arrow flight is the best investment bow shooters can make in terms of tightening up their groups. You must also concentrate on maintaining proper shooting form when paper-tuning. Consciously remain relaxed, keep your head up, relax your bow hand and release the shaft smoothly. Poor shooting form—particularly excess torque applied with the bow hand—can result in a less-than-perfect paper tear, leaving you wondering whether the problem lies with you or the bow.

Paper-tuning involves shooting your shafts through a sheet of paper at distances between 3 and 20 yards. The resulting holes in the paper—called tears—tell you what adjustments you need to make with your equipment. To do this test, you need some sort of rack to hold the paper. You could buy a commercial rack or you can make your own from plywood and cardboard. The paper should be about 24 by 24 inches and should be set up at shoulder height. Set up some sort of target butt behind the paper to catch the arrows.

When paper-tuning, I start out close to the paper, about six steps away. When the proper tear appears, I move back to 12 yards and shoot again. When things look good, I move back to 20 yards for my final paper test. Initially, your arrows will probably tear the paper at an angle rather than punch straight through it like a bullet. If the tear angles to the left or right, it's called fishtailing; if the tear is up or down, it's called porpoising. Usually you get a combination of the two.

The position of the nock point is the number-one concern when paper-tuning. If the paper tear is too low, it indicates a low nock point; if it's too high, a high nock point. Adjust the nock point as indicated, moving it a small amount ($1/4$ inch at the most) at a time until the hole is perfectly level or just a smidgen high. Holes like these show that the shaft rises slightly away from the arrow rest, a desirable trait because then the arrow will not strike the rest as it passes the riser.

Next, correct for left or right tears. Shafts that leave holes a bit left (for a right-handed shooter), indicate a weakly spined arrow. A combination of adjustments can help this problem. Decreasing the bow's draw weight is one modification. Increasing the weight of the rest's cushion plunger or the tension on the rest prongs (for shoot-through rests) is another. You can also move the rest in or out a bit as indicated by the position of the tear. If none of the above solves the problem, try using a stiffer shaft.

Shafts that leave holes to the right indicate too stiff of a spine (for right-handed archers). To remedy this, first try increasing the bow's draw weight or decreasing the tension of the cushion plunger or prong arms or both. As a last resort, try using shaft that is weaker in spine.

Record Your Bow's Measurements

At some point, paper-tuning will produce perfect or near-perfect bullet holes in the paper. When it does, take a few minutes to record your bow's measurements. Write down upper and lower limb tiller, nock height, distance between the nock set and bottom of the peep sight, draw weight and the distance of the arrow rest from the riser.

I like to paint a white mark on both my bow limb bolt and limb bolt adjustment screw so that

Bow Tuning Checklist

Record these measurements for future reference, once your bow is in tune.

- upper limb tiller
- lower limb tiller
- nock height
- distance between the nock set and bottom of the peep sight
- draw weight and the distance of the arrow rest from the riser
- paint a white mark on bow limb bolt
- paint a white mark limb bolt adjustment screw

Paper Tear Patterns

PAPER TUNING ARROW TEST

The Paper Tuning Arrow Test is a good basic bow tuning method for all three types of shooting styles—Recurve with finger release (RF), compound with finger release (CF) and compound with release aid (CR).

- Firmly attach a sheet of paper to a frame type rack approximately 24" x 24" (60 x 60 cm).
- Position the center of the paper about shoulder height with a target mat about 6 feet (1.8 m) behind the paper to stop the arrows.
- Stand approximately 6 feet (1.8 m) from the paper.
- Shoot a fletched arrow through the center of the paper with the arrow at shoulder height.
- Observe how the paper is torn.

 A. Tear A indicates good arrow flight. The point and fletching enter the same hole.

NOTE: *Try the following instructions in order, one at a time.*

B. Tear B indicates a low nocking point. To correct, raise the nocking point ¹/₁₆" (1.6 mm) at a time and repeat the procedure until the low vertical tear is eliminated.

C. Tear C indicates a high nocking point, clearance problem or (for release aid) a mismatched arrow spine. To correct, lower the nocking point ¹/₁₆" (1.6 mm) at a time until the high tear is eliminated. If the problem remains unchanged, the disturbance is probably caused by a lack of clearance or (for release aid) a mismatched arrow spine. CR only—if no clearance problem exists try:

1. A more flexible arrow rest blade or reducing downward spring tension on launcher rests.
2. Decreasing or increasing peak bow weight.
3. Reducing the amount the shaft overhangs the contact point of the arrow rest.
4. Using a stiffer arrow shaft.

NOTE: *The following instructions are for right-handed archers. Reverse for left-handed archers.*

RELEASE AID

 D. Tear D is uncommon for right-handed, CR archers. It generally indicates that the arrow rest position is too far to the right or that there is possible vane contact on the inside of the launcher rest.
To correct:

1. Move the arrow rest to the left in small increments.
2. Make sure the arrow has adequate clearance past the cable guard and cables.
3. Make sure your bow hand is well relaxed to eliminate excessive bow hand torque.

 E. For CR archers, a left or high-left tear is common and indicates a weak arrow or clearance problem. If a high-left tear exists, make sure you correct the nocking point first before proceeding further. To correct:

1. Move the arrow rest to the right.
2. Make sure your bow hand is well relaxed to eliminate excessive bow hand torque.
3. Decrease peak bow weight.
4. Choose a stiffer-spined arrow.

 F. Tear F shows more than one flight disturbance.
Combine the recommended procedures, correcting the vertical pattern (nocking point) first, then the horizontal. If you can't correct the arrow flight problem, have your local pro shop check the "timing" (rollover) of your eccentric wheels or cams.

- Depending on the type of arrow rest/mechanical release combinations, it may be necessary for archers using release aids to make adjustments opposite from those described above.
- Once you have achieved a good tune at 6 feet (1.8 m), move back 6 feet more and continue to shoot through the paper. This ensures that the tune is correct.

NOTE: *Correcting for Tear F with fingers follows the same procedures.*

FINGERS

 D. Tear D indicates a stiff arrow for RF, CF archers. To correct.

1. Increase peak bow weight.
2. Use a heavier arrow point and/or insert combination.
3. Use a lighter bow string.
4. Use a weaker-spined arrow.
5. Decrease cushion plunger tension, or use a weaker spring on "shoot around" rests.
6. CF only—Move the arrow rest to the right in small increments.

 E. Tear E indicates a weak arrow or clearance problem for RF, CF archers. To correct:

1. Check for clearance.
2. Decrease peak bow weight.
3. Use a lighter arrow point and/or insert combination.
4. Use a heavier bow string.
5. Use a stiffer-spined arrow.
6. Increase cushion plunger tension or use a stiffer spring on "shoot around" rests.
7. CF only—Move the arrow rest to the left in small increments.

Mark your limbs so that you can return them to the correct settings if they are ever moved.

when these two marks align, I know I've set my bow at exactly the right poundage. On some bows, limb bolts have a tendency to creep, and without this quick check your bow can sneak slightly out of tune without you ever knowing it.

With your bow's measurements written down, you have a reference chart that you can check in seconds with a bow square. I do this often to confirm quickly without shooting through paper that my bow is still in tune.

TESTING THE TUNE: A CONSTANT PROCESS

I believe you should constantly check your bow's tune. During the course of the year, I keep my paper-tuning rack handy. When I step out back to shoot a few practice arrows, if I haven't shot a shaft or two through the paper in a while, I do so. When my shafts produce a perfect tear on the first couple of shots, my confidence soars.

You should certainly recheck your bow's tune prior to heading afield. As the time nears for a hunting trip, spend an hour or two shooting at targets set at known distances so that you can check the bow's sights and reset them if necessary. This is also a good time to recheck all the bow's screws, bolts and accessories for looseness and breakage. During this session, shooting an arrow or two through paper to recheck the tune is quick and easy and will help you avoid an unexpected flyer that could cost you dearly.

Anything but glamorous, bow tuning can be downright boring and often frustrating. But without a precisely tuned bow, you'll never reach your full potential as a bow shot. Occasional flyers that

hit out of the target's kill zone will have you thinking you pulled the shot when really it was simply the way a bow that's not perfectly in tune will shoot. In extreme cases, I've seen shooters constantly adjust their bow sights to compensate for this less-than-perfect arrow flight when the answer is instead a quick retune of the bow. Consistent, dart-like arrow flight that permits you to reach your full potential as a bowhunter makes all the time and trouble it takes to tune your bow well worth the effort.

How a Pro Shop Can Help You

There's no better place to set up and tune a bow than your local archery pro shop. Here you'll find all the tools and small parts needed to get your bow ready to rock and roll: paper-tuning rack, target butts, a comfortable indoor range where wind and weather won't bother you.

Best of all, you'll be able to draw on the expertise of the resident pro, a person whose knowledge and skill in putting together and tuning a bow are unparalleled. If you buy your bow from the pro shop, they'll often throw in the setup and tuning assistance as part of the deal. If not, they'll charge you a small fee. But trust me—it's worth every penny.

I can't stress enough the importance of establishing a good relationship with your local pro shop. Besides, I just enjoy hanging out at the shop, swapping hunting stories and talking bowhunting. I bet you will too.

BROADHEAD GROUPING
AT DISTANCE

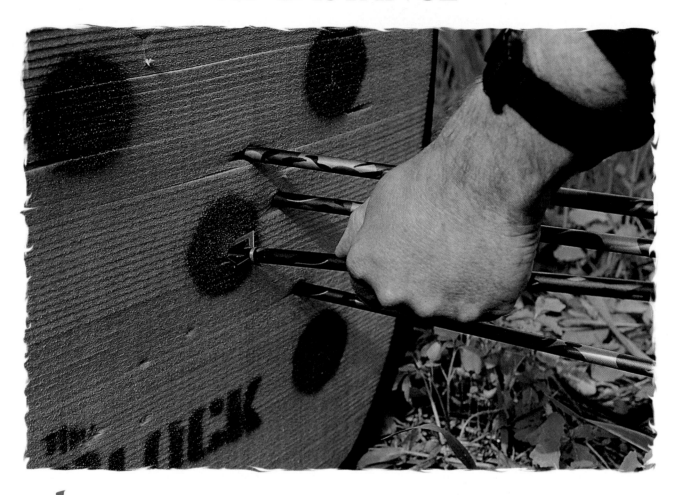

As a bowhunter, you're working toward superior performance with broadheads, not field and target points. After all, which type of arrow point will you be shooting at game?

To that end, I always tune my hunting bow with broadhead-tipped arrows before heading afield, and I set my sight pins accordingly. Many bowhunters mistakenly assume that their target points and broadheads will impact the target in the same place just because they weigh the same. In reality, this is rarely the case. Weight is not important. Achieving superb arrow flight with broadhead-tipped hunting shafts is important.

First I tune my bow with target points, then I sight it in. I may or may not practice with target points for a while, but once it's time to get ready for hunting season, I switch over and tune the bow with broadheads through paper, following the same step-by-step procedure used with field points and making the same corrections indicated by the tears in the paper.

Next, I go out and shoot groups at both short and long distances with my broadheads. The quality of these groups should be the final judge of whether or not your bow is ready for hunting season. I want my broadhead groups to be nearly as tight as those shot with field points. If they are not, then I may have additional tuning problems that need particular attention. Here's how to go about it.

Tuning With Broadheads

Begin with a large broadhead target set at 20 yards, a sight pin set for your practice points at 20 yards, and three broadhead-tipped shafts. On the target face, mark three same-size, easy-to-see spots with lots of room around them. Shoot just one shaft at each spot so you don't inadvertently cut the fletching of one shaft with the broadhead of another. Take your time, concentrate on your form and shoot one arrow at each spot. You probably won't hit the center of the spot, but that's okay. You're looking to see where each shaft hits in relation to the others near each spot.

If all three shafts hit near the same place in relation to their spot, you're set. Just adjust your sight pins for your broadhead-tipped shafts. If, however, they do not, you have some adjustments to make. The recommended sequence for these adjustments is: 1) try different nock point locations; 2) adjust the plunger or prong arm tension of the arrow rest, remaining conscious of possible fletch contact; 3) try a different draw weight. If all this doesn't work, some experts recommend a different arrow shaft size, but I've never gotten to that point.

Evaluating Broadheads

Rather than problems with the bow's tune, however, the trouble might be in the broadhead itself. When shooting broadhead groups, I always mark each arrow with a felt pen so I can identify it. Sometimes you'll find one or two broadhead-tipped shafts out of a dozen that simply won't consistently group with the others. This usually occurs due to a defect in the broadhead manufacture, generally (but not always) in the ferrule. If I have a shaft that doesn't fly well for a couple of shots, I'll switch the broadhead to a new arrow and shoot it again. If it still doesn't fly right on three or four different arrows, I discard that broadhead.

After successfully testing at 20 yards, I move back and set my sight pins for the distance I like them set at for most all of my hunting—20, 30, 40 and 50 yards. As I set my pins—and I generally take several hours over two days to get them set

the way I like them—I keep track of broadhead groups. When my hunting bow and broadhead-tipped arrow setup is shooting the way I want it to, even at 50 yards I have to shoot at different spots on the target to avoid cutting the fletch on a shaft or two.

Before hunting, I use an indelible felt pen to mark the broadhead and arrow shaft combination that is flying well with the same label so that they will always be matched together, even if I take the broadheads off during transportation. And prior to heading afield, I replace the now-dulled broadhead blades with fresh ones from a new pack.

3-D targets offer lifelike and essential practice with broadheads.

Bow Tuning Basics

Chapter 7

HOW TO SHOOT YOUR BOW

*E*very bowhunter's goal is to get close enough to the quarry to smell its breath. Unlike hunting with firearms, sneaking to within a football field won't do. Because of the difficulties of getting in the face of deer and other big-game animals, most bowhunters concentrate their time and effort along these lines. Sometimes they do so to the detriment of their shooting.

After all the hard work involved in spot-and-stalk hunting or in scouting the area, picking a stand site, then waiting for hours or even days for a deer to come along, when the time finally comes you want to be able to make that one shot count. But unless you have learned to shoot your bow correctly and paid your dues on the target range, you'll lack both the skills and the confidence necessary to turn shot opportunities consistently into punched tags.

And pay your dues you must. I've stressed before that with shooting a bow there are no shortcuts, no free lunches, no easy ways out. You must learn the proper way to shoot your bow, and you must spend time on the practice range honing your skills and tweaking your equipment to make sure the two of you will work in close harmony. It isn't like firearms hunting, where you can spend an hour on the rifle range before opening day making sure the gun is sighted in, then easily make the shot when the time comes. Every bowhunter needs to put in plenty of practice time.

A step-by-step method of learning the basics of bow shooting will help you be the best bow shot you can be. You'll also learn the right way and the wrong way to practice. Plus you'll find out about practice games to play. All this adds up, giving you the ability to make the shot when the chips are down.

Want to learn more? Then read on.

BOW SHOOTING
BY THE NUMBERS

*I*n the military, soldiers learn to do things "by the numbers." To them, it means there's a set method for doing things. Similarly, you can find success in shooting a bow by following this proven method.

FOUNDATIONS: STANCE & HANDS

In bow shooting, your foundation is your stance. Most skilled bow shooters prefer a sort of open stance, with the back foot set about 90 degrees to the target and the front foot set about 60 degrees. Spread your feet 12 to 18 inches apart (shoulder width, more or less) and get comfortable. Your torso should be straight up and down—don't lean forward or backward. As you lift the bow, you should not have to cock your head to see through your peep sight.

Relax your wrist and grip the handle lightly.

Proper hand position on the bow handle is critical. Regardless of how you grip the bow, you must grip the handle consistently each time. Variations in hand placement and pressure can cause inconsistencies in arrow flight. Keeping a natural, relaxed wrist, the major pressure should occur in the webbing between the thumb and forefinger. Lightly grip the bow with the index and middle fingers; don't "choke" the handle.

Drawing the Bow

To draw the bow, simply raise your bow arm into shooting position and smoothly draw the bowstring back to your anchor spot. Don't "cheat"—that is, lift the bow above the vertical to get it drawn back. If you have to cheat, reduce the draw weight until you can properly draw the string back. Over time your bow-pulling muscles will strengthen and you'll be able to pull more draw weight than in the beginning.

It is important to keep your bow arm relaxed during the draw. Once you get the bow up and drawn back, your bow arm should lock into place in a relaxed fashion. Your shoulder should be pulled down, forcing the humerus into the shoulder socket. You should also rotate your forearm so that your wrist is vertical, the best position for maximum bowstring clearance.

The key is to be comfortable and relaxed. Don't force things. A tense archer shoots poorly.

Don't cheat (top) while drawing your bow. Make sure you're able to draw without moving your bow from a "ready" position (bottom). The less movement the better while hunting.

Anchoring

A consistent anchor point is critical to accuracy. There is no "right" or "wrong" way to anchor, but you must anchor the same way, in the same place, *on every shot* to ensure consistency. When shooting with fingers, I like to place the tip of my index finger in the corner of my mouth. Some people place their thumb knuckle under their chin.

Anchor points with mechanical release aids vary by style of release. When shooting a wrist-strap caliper-type release—the most popular in use today—most shooters place the big knuckle of the thumb solidly under the rear of their jaw bone.

If you use a peep sight, as most present-day compound shooters do, touch the tip of your nose to the bowstring when you anchor. With the peep properly placed between the strands of the bowstring, this will do two things. First, it will allow you to see your sight pins clearly through the peep without cocking your head to one side or the other. Second, it will act as an additional anchor point, which helps reinforce your primary anchor point.

A consistent anchor point is crucial, with fingers or release aid.

Aiming

Aiming is not rocket science. You simply select the right sight pin for the distance, place it in the center of the peep sight, put it on the center of the target, hold it steady for a moment and release.

Again, consistency is the key. A smart bowhunter places his or her pin on the target the same way every time. Some like to line up the shot, then move the sight pin up from the bottom of the target to the correct location before releasing. Others like to come from the top down. Both methods work well, but you'll shoot better if you do it the same way every time. It's also important to move the pin on target smoothly instead of in a herky-jerky motion.

You'll find that, try as you might, it is impossible to hold the sight pin completely steady on the target. Though the pin will bounce and jump

Practice shooting between pins for odd distances.

around, don't fight it. Most top shooters let the sight pin float over and around the target, releasing the arrow when it floats over the right spot. You'll also find that you can't focus your eye on both the target and the sight pin at the same time. You'll shoot best if you focus on the sight pin, not the animal. As I settle my sight pin, I focus on the target first, picking the spot on the animal I want to hit. I then let my subconscious remember that spot and focus on the sight pin as I place it precisely where I want my arrow to go.

On the target range, you'll shoot from marked distances that correspond to the common sight pin settings of 20, 30, 40 and 50 yards. In the field, you'll often find that you'll be shooting at an animal that is an odd distance away. Instead of 20 or 30 yards away, it might be at 25 yards, for example. If you use a common pin-type bow sight, you'll then have to shoot between the pins.

On these shots, I simply split the difference between my pins when aiming. Instead of putting the 20-yard pin on the spot I want to hit, I raise it slightly above the spot, keeping the 30-yard pin just below it. This places the space between the pins vertically dead on the target. Also, by drawing an imaginary line between the two pins, I can line up the shot horizontally. This may sound weird at first, but it works.

RELEASING THE ARROW

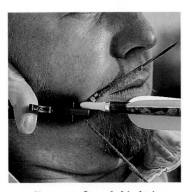

Keep your finger behind trigger until you're ready to shoot.

A smooth, consistent bowstring release is also critical to accurate shooting. If you shoot with your fingers, simply relax the fingers and let the string go, smoothly slipping away. Do not throw the string hand open or pluck the string like a guitar, which are two common mistakes.

Using a mechanical release

aid is the most consistent, error-free way to release a bowstring. With the simple squeeze of a trigger or press of a button, the release turns the string loose with the same amount of pressure every shot.

Release shooting isn't a no-brainer though. It is easy to punch or jerk the trigger or button, which defeats the purpose of the exercise. Approach the triggering mechanism the same way every time. To prevent accidentally setting off the trigger of my release prematurely, I keep my trigger finger or thumb behind the trigger when drawing the bow, not placing it on the trigger itself until I'm settling my sight pin onto my spot.

FOLLOWING THROUGH

Don't forget to follow through. Dropping your bow or forcing it to the side before the arrow has cleared the rest will send the shaft off target. To follow through, concentrate on continuing to aim at the target after you have released the string.

Follow through properly: Continue to aim at the target after you've released.

Though it sounds simple, most archers find that follow-through is the most difficult part of bow shooting. In the excitement of shooting at a big-game animal, most of us—including me—tend to drop that bow out of the way so we can watch the arrow strike the target. That's a formula for failure. Instead, concentrate on keeping your bow arm straight, looking for the spin of the fletching through your peep sight. A conscious follow-through is necessary for virtually every good bow shot I know.

Different Practice Targets

Serious bowhunters have several different types of targets for practice. Why? Because your practice sessions will have different purposes, and different types of targets provide a way of getting the most from your practice while minimizing cost.

Hay bale.

The most common target type, a basic **target butt**, can be everything from a bale of hay or straw to a large, round, commercially made butt set on a tripod stand. You can face target butts with a variety of paper aiming points including bull's eyes, diamonds, squares and even drawings of game animals.

Bag targets feature a woven burlap or nylon cover and a thick filling—often cotton—that is either freestanding or stands in place on a frame of aluminum tubing. Designed for practice-tipped arrows only, the best bag targets can withstand many hundreds—some many thousands—of shots before wearing out. Lower-grade bag targets are designed for low-poundage bows shooting aluminum arrows, while the best can handle any shaft, including carbon arrows shot from high-poundage bows.

Bag target.

You can shoot **foam targets** with either practice points or broadheads. Again, there are different models, with some designed to stop only aluminum arrows and others able to take carbon shafts. These target types are great for

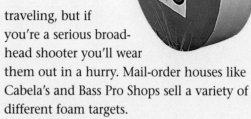
Foam target.

traveling, but if you're a serious broadhead shooter you'll wear them out in a hurry. Mail-order houses like Cabela's and Bass Pro Shops sell a variety of different foam targets.

Every bowhunter needs a high-quality **broadhead target**. The key is finding one that

Broadhead target.

can take a lot of shooting before wearing out, yet permits you to pull your arrows without the strength of Hercules.

Three-dimensional (3-D) targets offer the best arrow-stopping ability and allow you to practice on a life-sized replica of a game animal. The best have replaceable cores, so when you shoot them out you can easily replace them without breaking the bank. These expensive targets make superb practice tools.

See page 172 for target manufacturer information.

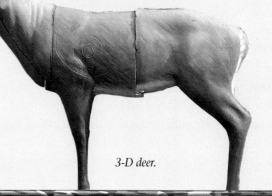
3-D deer.

How to Shoot Your Bow

Proper Practice Techniques

You've set up your bow with the right accessory package for bowhunting, then tuned it and sighted it in. You already know how to shoot it properly. Now it's time to begin practicing for the upcoming season.

Simple, right? Well, yes and no. There is a right way and a wrong way to practice shooting. The right way will increase your skill level, knowledge of the nuances of your individual bow-and-arrow setup and your confidence. The wrong way can actually impair your shooting skills.

What's the right way?

The Right Stuff

The most important advice anyone can give you about practicing your bow shooting is this: Take your time and concentrate. The best field shots I know play a little game with themselves.

They know that bowhunters rarely get a second shot at an animal and that the entire hunting trip boils down to the ability to make one arrow count. To that end, when they practice, they shoot every arrow as if it were the only arrow they'll shoot at an animal during the entire hunting season.

They take their time and concentrate on every step of the shot sequence—standing correctly, smoothly drawing the bow, cleanly releasing the arrow and following through. They know that if they blow it, all is lost. They also know following the proper shooting technique and not rushing through the shot will make the shot work.

One buddy of mine goes so far as to tape a small reminder onto the inside of his upper bow limb, where his eyes will automatically pick it up as he comes to full draw and looks for his sight pins. It reads simply, "Relax. Pick a spot. Follow through." It helps him remember the things he must do to make the shot.

HOW SOON SHOULD I BEGIN PRACTICING?

Most of us, for a variety of reasons, can't practice with our bows on a daily basis all year long. I do make a conscious effort to begin shooting a little bit three or four months prior to hunting season, which gives me plenty of time to iron out kinks in my form as well as find and fix problems with my tackle.

As the season gets closer, I step up my practice sessions. It is unethical simply to grab your bow out of the closet, shoot a few practice arrows a week or two before opening day, then head afield. We all owe it both to the game we hunt and to our fellow bowhunters to take enough time to prepare our shooting skills so that when the time comes, we can make an accurate shot and a clean, humane kill.

Once I begin practicing in earnest, I try to shoot a few arrows at least every

other day. Shooting a bow is an athletic skill, and the way to be your best is to keep your form sharp and your muscles tuned.

SHOOTING WITH YOUR EYES CLOSED

At a pro shop one day, I watched the resident professional give a new archer her first shooting lesson. To my surprise, he set the target 10 feet in front of her, then had her draw the bow with her eyes closed. He lined her up on the hay bales, then had her release the arrow. They did this for 30 minutes, then quit.

What the heck? How can you be a good shooter if you can't even see the target? But he was instilling in her the importance of good shooting form. He helped her concentrate on relaxing, squeezing the shot off and following through. Such practice pays off even after you've become Robin Hood. Often before a serious practice session I'll shoot a dozen arrows with my eyes closed, just to warm my muscles up and to remind myself that, paraphrasing the old saying, "It's the form, stupid!"

Eyes-closed practice promotes good shooting habits.

How to Shoot Your Bow

Long Distance Practice

*E*very year, beginning bowhunters ask me how far away I shoot on the practice range. When I tell them I have a 60-yard pin set on my hunting bow sight, they look at me like I'm nuts. "Why would I want to shoot that far," they ask, "when I hunt whitetails from a treestand and my shots are never longer than 25 steps?"

First off, I never begin practicing at 60 yards. Months before the season begins, I may spend a week or more never shooting beyond the 20-yard line. I want to make sure I've got both my equipment and myself in good working order before challenging myself with long-distance shooting.

As you become more skilled in your shooting, move farther away from the target. Soon you'll be able to make consistently good shots at 40 yards or more. Practicing at longer distances will effectively force you to concentrate on every facet of accurately shooting your bow. Longer ranges will exponentially magnify even small flaws in your shooting form. The bull's eye looks much smaller at 40 yards and beyond, and the minuscule movements of your bow arm will cause your sight pins to jump all over the target at these distances. To make these shots, you really have to pay attention and use proper shooting form and technique.

Once you begin making good shots at 40 yards, you'll be surprised at how easy those 20-yarders become. I firmly believe that bowhunters should practice shooting well past the distances at which they anticipate taking shots at game. Not that you should ever shoot at an animal past your own comfort zone—it's just that once you have mastered basic shooting form and skills, long-distance practice is the best way to improve your overall ability to make the shot at any distance.

During practice, start close and move back as you become more comfortable. Long-distance practice makes the practical-range shots seem easy.

Too Much of a Good Thing?

What's the best way to master bow shooting? Simply stated, consistency without overpracticing. Surprising to some, it is easy to practice too much with your bow. With over-practice you can effectively develop sloppy shooting habits. Your arm, back and shoulder muscles will become sore and fatigued with too much shooting. You can also lose your concentration after too many practice arrows. When that happens, you'll see your groups open up and your shooting form falter, which leads to a lack of confidence and bad shooting habits.

When you feel tired, take a break. Most beginners have trouble shooting more than 20 to 40 arrows before fading. After I've been shooting for a few months, I find I can shoot, at most, 80 to 100 arrows in a day's time before I tire. It is also a good idea not to shoot a lot of arrows day in and day out. Taking a day off helps your muscles—and, just as important, your mind—to recover.

When I begin my own serious preseason practice sessions four months before opening day, I shoot only a dozen arrows the first few times out. As time goes by, the number of arrows I shoot during practice sessions increases. I also try never to shoot a lot of arrows two days in a row. If I shoot 50 to 80 shafts one day, the next day I might shoot only 10 to 15—if I shoot at all.

Relax

Take your time between practice shots. Shooting a bow is not a game of speed but as much a game of calculation and mental preparation as it is physically making the shot. I like to shoot an arrow, then take a minute or two before the next shot.

Relax is the key word when you practice. You need to be calm and under control to hit a little kill zone like the one on this 3-D turkey.

This gives me time to relax my muscles and go through my mental checklist of proper shooting form. When you shoot too quickly, it is easy to get into a groove of making the same mistakes over and over until they have become ingrained and thus difficult habits to break.

Just like highly trained athletes, who have their good days and their bad days, so too will you when it comes to shooting your bow. Some days it seems that your arrows magically fly to the center of the target. On other days, it's tough to find your posterior with both hands. Don't worry about it. When I'm having "one of those days," I quit shooting and go do something else. There's no use fighting it, so why try? It's better to retreat and come back a day or two later, mind refreshed and muscles relaxed.

One final note: During practice sessions, never be satisfied with mediocre accuracy results. At 20 yards, you should be able to place your broadheads consistently in a 2-inch circle. At 40 yards, a 4-inch group is my goal. At 50 yards, I try to get each and every shot into a 6-inch circle. This kind of precision shooting will translate into your broadhead-tipped shaft finding the vitals of your quarry every time, regardless of the excitement and adrenaline rush.

How to Shoot Your Bow

REALISTIC HUNTING PRACTICE

Once you've gotten your bow set up and shooting darts, your sight pins set and your shooting form working, it's time to move from the static practice range to practice that closely resembles actual bowhunting.

Don't get me wrong; regular practice on a flat course with targets set at marked distances is not bad for you. During the course of the hunting season I do most all of my practice shooting on target ranges just like that. But to become an effective bow shot on game, you need to incorporate some realistic hunting practice into your regimen.

BAD-WEATHER PRACTICE

Practicing your bow shooting under ideal conditions is great. It helps you build confidence, fine-tune your tackle and perfect your shooting form. Such practice may also make you think you're a better field shot than you really are. How so? Because until you throw in some adverse weather conditions, you won't know how well you can shoot.

For example, most of my buddies wouldn't be caught dead practicing their shooting on a cold, windy, rainy day. Heck, why go outside when there's a comfortable couch, a ball game on TV and a heater inside? And while I like all of that stuff, I make a point of practicing my shooting on at least a few days when the weather's crummy. That's the only way to find out how much the wind pushes your bow around, if rain and snow ice up your arrows or plug your peep sight, or if moisture causes a cable slide to squeak.

This year, make it a point to get in some bad-weather practice. It can pay big dividends when that buck of a lifetime finally shows himself on "one of those days."

Sooner or later you'll want or need to hunt in the rain (left). Practice in it to be ready when a bad-weather shot comes. Same thing goes when the season is old, the weather frigid (right). If you haven't shot in months, how will you ever make a shot now? Keep shooting, all season long, in all weather.

Stalking Practice

*T*o hunt out West, you have to learn how to walk softly, heel to toe, carefully avoiding crackling sticks or scuffing your toes against rocks and root balls. You have to learn to walk slowly—so slowly that you

Stalking skills don't just happen. You must learn and practice them.

think you'll never get anywhere—pausing often to look and listen, keeping your head up, scanning the countryside for the telltale flicker of an ear or tail, a piece of antler, a horizontal backline in a sea of vertical brush.

Treestand whitetail hunters can also benefit from stalking skills. Who doesn't want to slip in to the stand undetected? Such skills are not natural to us, so we must practice them. You don't just sneak quietly through the woods by thinking you want to; like anything else, it takes practice.

STUMP SHOOTING

When you're in the field on a bowhunt, continue practicing daily. I regularly fly a small, high-density ethafoam target into remote hunting camps in the far North by bush plane so I can shoot a few practice broadhead-tipped arrows every day. I always carry several Bludgeon and Judo points with me, using them for stump shooting at tufts of grass, old rotten stumps and such all day long.

Stump shooting is one of the best in-the-field practice games you can play. Besides being lots of fun, it also has two major benefits. One, it helps keep shooting muscles toned up and loose. And two, it helps you learn to judge distance accurately in the actual terrain you're hunting without the use of a rangefinder.

Stump shooting practice also helps me know what kind of rhythm I'm in on a particular day. I spent many years in highly competitive athletics and learned that even the best athletes have their good and bad days. If I'm having a bad day while practicing, I often stop and take some time off to try to work the kinks out until I'm back in the groove. If I still feel a bit shaky, my personal maxi-

mum shooting distance shrinks accordingly. Here's an example.

I was stalking a big black bear one day in coastal Alaska, coming down from above him and hoping for a close shot. I sneaked relatively easily

Having confidence to make a clean shot will greatly increase if you have practiced stump shooting in the field while on your hunt.

to within 35 yards of the coal-black bruin but didn't shoot. My stump shooting that day had left me a little nervous of a shot at a bear at that distance, and coupled with a strong breeze that made it difficult to hold my bow arm steady, I elected to try to get closer. At 25 yards the wind suddenly shifted, and because I had shrunk my own personal shooting distance on that particular day, my "gimme" became a "goner."

That sort of thing used to bother me a lot. When it happens today, though, I know I've done my best and stayed within my personal effective shooting range on that particular day. In doing so, I did not take a shot in which I didn't have complete confidence.

And that's the way it should be. Every time.

What Is Specificity Training?

*E*xercise physiologists use the term specificity training to describe workout regimens that help train athletes to perform a specific task to their maximum potential. For example, while sprinters may do some upper-body weight training, they concentrate on building up those muscles and organs that most help them when they run—their legs, lungs and heart.

One way we bowhunters can do the same thing is to incorporate into our regular program exercises that will specifically help us shoot better. For example, strengthen your back and your shooting arm, which work to draw the bow, and your bow arm, which holds the bow up.

To strengthen the back, do exercises in the gym like bent and seated rowing, pull-ups and pull-downs. Using light dumbbells, hold your arms at your sides, then lift them out in front of you and hold them steady—as if you were holding your bow up at full draw. If you're going on a mountain hunt, work on your climbing muscles by jogging or hiking up and down stadium steps or hills near your home, or work out vigorously on the stair-step machine.

Create your practice setup to mirror your actual hunting setup.

Another way to train is to practice shooting your bow to replicate the kind of hunting you'll be doing. If you hunt

Get in shape or miss out. It's that simple.

from a treestand and usually take shots between 15 and 25 yards, for example, make sure you practice shooting that way before the season begins. Either set a treestand and shoot from it or climb up on a hill or some sort of raised platform, trying to match as closely as you can the height of your treestand. I often practice off the second-story deck of my house. If you're a spot-and-stalk hunter who spends his time on the ground, practice shooting over and under branches and brush, from your knees, with your torso twisted at odd angles and so on.

You get the idea. By specifically training yourself to make those shots you'll most commonly encounter during the season, you'll be better prepared to make them when the time comes. And that's what it's all about.

HOW FAR IS TOO FAR?

With the possible exception of religion, politics or the merits of different brands of fine sippin' whiskey, few things can heat up a bowhunting camp debate like the subject of the farthest distances at which a skilled bowhunter should actually take a shot at a big-game animal.

CONSIDER THIS

It had been a close-but-no-cigar week of elk hunting in the Madison Mountains of southwestern Montana. The September weather had been beautiful and warm, and I had been into bulls every day. I could have shot a couple of $2^1/_2$-year-old raghorns, but I was holding out for a crack at one of the real dandies I'd seen herding his harem into the dark timber at first light. I had yet to loose an arrow.

On the last evening, after a stick-and-move calling confrontation that had taken more than an hour, a very large 5x5 bull stepped out into an open meadow not 40 yards distant. He stood there, perfectly broadside, and bugled and tore up the muddy grass in a rut-crazed frenzy. But when I raised my bow and came to full draw, the sun had dropped just far enough behind the peaks that I couldn't get a clear picture of my sight pin against the bull's dark, mud-crusted chest. And so I softly let the arrow down and enjoyed the show until pitch dark, my hunting trip now over and an expensive—and unpunched—nonresident elk tag burning a hole in my pocket.

It was a fitting and wonderful end to one of the finest weeks of wilderness elk hunting I have ever experienced. It also serves as a good illustration of my philosophy of shooting at game with my bow:

If I'm not absolutely 100 percent sure I can hit the animal square in the chest, I don't shoot. I make no exceptions for antler size or for the money invested in licenses and tags, airline tickets and guide service—or in my own sweat and blisters.

A 40-yard shot is well within my shooting abilities, one that I've made many times. I practice diligently at much longer ranges, and if everything is right I wouldn't hesitate to take an even longer shot at game with complete confidence.

The key phrase in that last paragraph is "if everything is right." With that big Montana bull, everything was perfect except the dim light. The chances were maybe 60-40 that I could have hit him in the lungs, but 60-40 isn't good enough for me. Nor should it be good enough for you.

Now consider this scenario: We were hunting mule deer in the sagebrush foothills of northern New Mexico. The bowhunters were from the East, with some treestand hunting experience but none in the way of open-country hunting. Back home, the Eastern archers had not taken the time to practice the skills need to take a buck here—stalking silently, moving as the game dictates you must,

extending your personal shooting distances—and as the week wore on, it was apparent that it would take a miracle for them to fill their tags.

In frustration, they began flinging arrows at bucks anywhere from 40 to 75 yards away. One bowhunter shot 17 times, another a dozen times, to no avail. Thankfully, neither hit a deer poorly.

KNOW YOUR PERSONAL ABILITIES

Each bowhunter has his or her own shooting ability. No one else shoots at game exactly the same way or with the exact same degree of skill as you do. No two bowhunters perceive the target identically, even under identical conditions. It's an individual thing. One of the most important things in all of bowhunting is for each individual to recognize his or her own shooting abilities—and inabilities—and stay within them at all times.

I know bowhunters who regularly take game in the wide-open spaces of the West at 60 yards and more, their arrows slicing through the center of the animal's chest cavity as neat as you please. Yet these bowhunters hesitate to tell anyone how far

Know your limits: Don't shoot at an animal that's not within your comfort range.

their shot was, hoping to avoid ridicule and accusations of being poor sportsmen. In reality, these individuals have earned the right to take longer shots through constant practice, careful bow tuning, uncompromising confidence in their equipment, a familiarity with the terrain they hunt and an intimate knowledge of the habits of the animals they pursue. In fact, they have more of a right to take a 50-yard shot at game than many less-skilled bowhunters have to shoot at half that distance.

Skilled, experienced bowhunters know what we all must learn and remember: that each shot presents a unique set of problems to overcome, distance being only one of them.

On my elk hunt, poor light was the determining factor. On another occasion—a bedded mule deer buck on a grassy slope—the 40 yards my rangefinder told me was the exact distance between us was in no way the reason I didn't shoot. A strong, gusting cross wind of perhaps 30 miles an hour would have pushed my arrow to the side a distance of which I was unsure, so I tried to sneak closer to minimize the wind's effect. Impatience made me hurry, and at 25 yards I rolled a softball-sized rock right into that buck's back. Had I been bowling I would have been in the chips. As it was, I had an excellent view of that 28-incher's backside as he bounded off into the dark timber.

A rangefinder eliminates the guesswork on distance.

EXPERIENCE: THE KEY TO SUCCESS

Experience is the most important piece of equipment a bowhunter can take into the field. None of the terrific, new high-tech doodads the industry has made available to us over the past several years can take the place of your own ability to size up each situation, make a set of judgments based on your own experiences and then decide whether or not the time is right to take the shot.

Experience is comprised of many different things. It's time spent in the woods, both during and out of the hunting season. It's being around the game you're hunting, acquiring an intangible feel for the animal and an ability to anticipate its actions. It's time spent honing your hunting skills, including stalking, sneaking, moving quietly and

more. It's familiarity with your chosen bow-and-arrow setup, how it draws, how long you can hold it at full draw, just how it settles in your hand, the trajectory of your arrows. It's how well you can judge distance to the target. And it's how well you shoot your bow with broadhead-tipped arrows.

ANOTHER KEY: ESTIMATING RANGE

Tests conducted by the military have shown that the average person cannot accurately judge distances over 40 yards. And as any bowhunter knows, thanks to the horrible arcing trajectory of arrows shot from even the fastest hunting compound bows, without a precise knowledge of how far away the target is, you're going to miss the shot. Period.

How to Shoot Your Bow

Using 5-yard increments will help you in the field, where yard markers are not present.

Practice in judging distance will help you, however. During the off-season, I try to guess distances to objects around town. How far away is that street sign? That light pole? That car? Then I pace it off to check my guess. Over time, it's amazing how this helps.

But I don't stop there. When I'm in the field hunting, I am constantly guesstimating distances to inanimate objects—tree trunks, bushes, rocks and so on. Again, I validate my guesses by either pacing them off or using a rangefinder. This invaluable practice helps me accurately gauge distance in the terrain in which I'm hunting. Trust me on this one—distances appear to be different in different types of terrain.

TREESTAND HUNTING

Whenever possible, when hunting from a treestand, I carefully measure the range from my stand to several different, easily recognizable objects in the woods around me. I try to guess where the deer will be coming from and how they will be traveling, picking objects along these routes to range. At times I'll even jot those distances down in a pocket notebook and post the page on a limb at head height so I can use it for quick and easy reference in the heat of the hunt.

You can gauge distance one of two ways. The first is simply to pace it off before climbing into the stand. This works well if it's an afternoon stand or if you have preset the stand before hiking to it in the dark. If you're climbing into a new stand in the dark, though, you won't have time to pace things off. That's the time to use your rangefinder.

Since most treestand hunting involves extremely close-range shooting, estimating distance isn't as critical as it is in spot-and-stalk situations, where the terrain continually varies and shots can be anywhere from point blank to way out there. Still, knowing the exact distance to the target is one of the most important factors in placing the broadhead in the boiler room.

BREAK DISTANCES DOWN

When eyeballing range, don't try to be super precise. No one can call it to the yard every time. Instead, measure it in easy-to-understand increments. I use 5 yards as my baseline measurement. For example, instead of looking at a deer and saying, "He's 43 yards away," I tell myself, "He's between 40 and 45 yards away." That means I shoot between the pins, placing the gap between my 40- and 50-yard pins on his chest. With my current bow-and-arrow setup, when the range is under 25 yards, all I have to do is put my 20-yard pin on the chest and shoot. The trajectory is such that I'm going to hit him in the vitals every time.

Also, when looking at long distances over broken ground, I try to use measurement increments I know well. For example, I can pretty much tell when something is 20 yards away. If game is out past 20 yards, I try to use the terrain and flora between the deer and myself to help me. I might say to myself, "okay, that pine tree is 20 yards; the big rock beyond that is about 10 yards, and the trail the deer is standing on is maybe 5 yards past that. That makes it 35 yards." That's what I shoot for.

Rangefinders: Don't Leave Home Without One

Because misguessing the distance to the target is the number-one reason experienced bowhunters miss shots at game, a higher-quality bowhunting rangefinder is one of the best investments you can make.

You'll find two kinds of rangefinders: coincidence and laser. Coincidence units, popularized by Ranging, Inc., work on the principle of triangulation. They have two windows and a system of prisms and lenses that produces two images you see when you look through the viewfinder. You simply turn a precalibrated dial—stopping when the two images coincide and become one—then read the distance off the dial. With a bit of practice, you can use these types of units quite accurately. I used a Ranging 80/2 for years with good success.

Coincidence rangefinder.

But today the laser rangefinder is really the way to go. Laser units function by sending out a beam of light—the laser beam—which reflects off the target object. The unit mathematically translates the precise distance between the unit and the target from the amount of time it takes for the beam to go out and return to the rangefinder unit.

Today's laser rangefinders are precise to within plus or minus 1 yard at distances well beyond what any bowhunter will ever shoot. Compact and portable with a neck strap or a soft belt pouch, they work on a standard 9-volt battery that will give hundreds of "shots" before wearing down. Laser rangefinders can also take a fair amount of field abuse and keep on ticking.

Laser rangefinder.

The best units I've used to date are from Bushnell, including their Yardage Pro 400 and my favorite, the Yardage Pro Compact 600. I've taken these units into weather ranging from 100°F to minus 50°F, without a problem. Brunton, Simmons and Tasco also offer reasonably priced units, while companies like Swarovski and Leica make outstanding combination binocular/rangefinder units costing several thousand dollars. The others range in price from around $200 to $300.

As Clint Eastwood said in one of the Dirty Harry movies, "A man's got to know his limitations." I do. While I still work hard at being able to eyeball distance, whenever possible I use my laser rangefinder. Why take a chance?

Virtual Bowhunting

Adecade ago, dreaming, planning and tinkering with our equipment was all we bowhunters could do in the off season. But today we can go bowhunting 365 days a year, right in our own homes or backyards. It doesn't take a lot of scouting or planning. An entire hunt may take just a couple of hours. We can do it on the weekend or in the evening after work. It really doesn't matter how bad the weather is, or even if the sun has gone down—we can do it after dark too.

Welcome to the world of virtual bowhunting, one of the best forms of realistic hunting practice there is.

Virtual bowhunting is done in one of two ways: utilizing one of the innovative new interactive video games that features videotaped scenes of live game animals moving through their natural habitat, or shooting at life-sized 3-D targets of animals.

INTERACTIVE VIDEO SYSTEMS

Three major manufacturers produce interactive video systems today:

Dart International, Inc. (800-869-6377), which began the revolution; TechnoHunt, by Advanced Interactive Systems (800-441-4487); and Visual Concepts (573-885-4619). The games are set up in

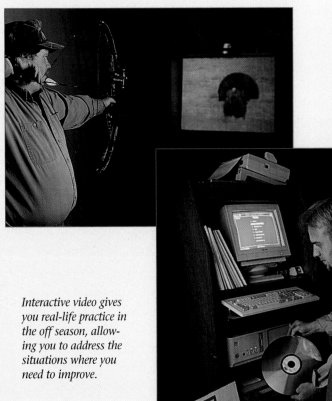

Interactive video gives you real-life practice in the off season, allowing you to address the situations where you need to improve.

participating archery dealers' pro shops, where you can go and try them out for a few dollars per round. You can call each company to find the closest participating dealer.

The Dart and TechnoHunt systems are very similar. When you step up to the line, you can choose between a number of different scenarios on laser disks (the Dart system offers more than 900 different video scenarios, for example), each with audio for added realism. The shooter has 20 to 30 seconds to shoot an arrow equipped with a special blunt tip at the video screen. When the arrow hits the screen and bounces off, the scene freezes. Each shot is scored based on where the shaft hits. To get the maximum number of points, you must hit the vital heart/lung area. Scores are displayed on the screen and recorded in the game's computer database. Following that shot, there is a brief pause, then another animal in a different scene appears and you're ready to go again.

The VAC System is a bit different. Shooters use their own arrows with their own practice points, and the arrows actually stick into the system's screen. Shooters score their own arrows in this game.

Virtual bowhunting in the form of interactive video systems is a superb and fun way to stay sharp during the off-season. A growing number of archery pro shops and retailers are adding these systems to their shops. The companies producing the systems continue to upgrade them and introduce new and different video disks, so you'll never get bored shooting the same old thing over and over again.

3-D Targets

In my mind, there is absolutely no better way to practice for actual bowhunting than shooting at life-sized three-dimensional targets designed to replicate the specific animals you'll be hunting.

There are 3-D targets of just about every animal you can think of, from small game to turkeys to deer, all the way up to African game. Many 3-D targets have removable core "kill zones" so that when these bull's eye areas have been shot out you can easily replace them.

Try 3-D target shooting alone or with friends, on courses set up specifically for serious 3-D shooting or informal setups put together by yourself or with your buddies. Many archery clubs across the country have 3-D courses established for their members, but they will allow the general public to shoot the course for a fee.

For general bowhunting practice, there are several little games you can play with 3-D targets to help improve your skills as a field shot.

Each year I set a 60-yard pin on my hunting bows, primarily to take advantage of the 60-yard field course set over open, flat ground in my backyard. Both standard and 3-D targets are set from 15 to 60 yards, and I begin my practice sessions there. Under these controlled conditions I wring the kinks out of my shooting form, get my bow-shooting muscles tuned up and generally get a good feel for my equipment and myself. Here I can check my bows over closely for technical problems and correct them. I can also resight my bow in until I know exactly where it will shoot at a given distance over flat ground.

Once I'm comfortable, I add sessions on a small simulated hunting course. I have a couple of treestands set up from which I practice shooting from an elevated platform at 3-D targets set at various distances at various angles.

I also set my 3-D targets to simulate spot-and-stalk hunting. The targets are set over broken ground, with shots taken over small gullies, uphill and downhill and through brush. I practice drawing my bow and shooting from my knees, as well as kneeling and standing with my body twisted and contorted at a variety of angles, which are positions I frequently find myself shooting from when stalking.

You don't need a herd of 3-D animals. Just one target will do. Set it up in an open area, then move your shooting stations around it, varying both the distance and shot angles.

Because these targets are built to last, pulling your arrows out of them—especially when you're shooting broadheads—can be a seemingly Herculean task. Two things will help make arrow removal easier. First, apply a light coating of liquid dish soap or a liquid silicone compound to the front third of your arrow shaft before shooting into a 3-D target. The slippery coating will help your shaft slide out of the target as neat as can be. And an inexpensive product, the Gorilla Grip, fits in the palm of your hand and wraps around the arrow shaft to give you a solid hold while pulling the shaft from the target. It works great.

3-D targets provide lifelike body sizes for practicing.

A 3-D range presents many different circumstances that you many encounter while afield.

Replicate hunting conditions as closely as possible, even shooting from your treestand and taking odd-angle shots.

How to Shoot Your Bow

Chapter 8

MAKING THE
SHOT ON GAME

*I*t's a frosty morning and the sun's not yet peeking over the eastern horizon when you first see him. His blocky body is dark, his neck swollen and his antlers tall and heavy. He's 75 yards out but on a trail that should bring him within 20 yards of your treestand.

It's show time.

Isn't it amazing how many thoughts can run through your mind at a time like this? You wonder why, despite those insulated bibs and long underwear, your knees are knocking. "Control yourself!" you silently scream. You quickly remember all those hours spent on the practice range, honing your skills and fine-tuning your equipment. You think, "Yeah, I've dreamed about this moment for years, and I'm ready." And you're wondering, how should I tell my buddies about the big buck I killed—just blurt it out, or torture them a little first?

The buck keeps coming, and you keep thinking, "Lord, I hope he doesn't change course. Please turn broadside when you get here! How much of an angle should I give him before shooting? Just how far is that tree on the trail I hit with my range finder a dozen times before now? I can't remember! Should I let him walk past me or take him as he gets even? When should I draw? I don't want him to see me."

And then he's on top of you, and you instinctively come to full draw. "Holy smokes, he didn't see me draw!" you think. And don't forget to aim a bit low on his chest. Okay, now. Relax. Pick a spot. Get a good sight picture. Follow through.

And then the arrow flies free. It's all a blur after that, the shaft sizzling on its way, the buck jumping and running off, the woods, noisy for a moment, suddenly as quiet as a tomb. Your heart is trying to beat its way out of your chest and your knees are really knocking now. You hang your bow up and try to calm down. "Man," you wonder, "did I get him?"

Shooting at game is nothing like target practice. There's no room for error, no mulligan now. This is when all your practice and preparation pays off. You have to know where to aim and when to drop the string. You must understand arrow trajectory. And while "buck fever" won't ever go away, you have to learn to control it at the moment of truth.

Show time. There's nothing like it on earth.

SHOT PLACEMENT

We've discussed in detail the importance of fine-tuning your bow-and-arrow setup, working on your shooting form and using only strong broadheads with blades so sharp they scare you. You already know that a broadhead-tipped arrow kills by creating massive hemorrhaging as well as causing organ failure when you hit your game square in the heart or lungs. You have to place your shaft in the animal's vitals to kill it cleanly and it is your solemn responsibility to do everything in your power to make this happen every time.

WHEN TO SHOOT

Bowhunters have lots of decisions to make, ranging from choosing equipment and clothing to deciding where to set their stands. But the most important decision you'll ever make as an ethical bowhunter is when and when not to shoot at game.

At first glance, deciding when to turn an arrow loose seems simple. When the animal appears within your comfortable shooting range, you shoot it. But upon closer examination, it's not quite so simple.

Because each situation is different, there are no hard-and-fast rules. What is a good shot opportunity for you may not be a good shot for me. Always remember that just because an animal stands within range doesn't mean you automatically have a shot. Far from it. A shot I never took at a great buck is a prime example.

As dark approached on the eighth and last day of a tough hunt in northeastern Kansas, he came, seemingly out of nowhere. I'd been dreaming of this buck all my life. He was a blocky-bodied, swollen-necked 8-pointer with long, massive tines, big eye guards and main beams that almost touched just over his nose. He came up from an oak bottom and was on a path to cross through the saddle in which I'd set my climbing stand that morning.

He came with 21 yards of my stand and stopped broadside. But the wind was swirly, and he knew something was up. In the fading light I couldn't clearly see all the little twigs and branches between us. Even though I was 75 percent sure I could slip an arrow through the maze, those odds weren't good enough for me. Rather than risk wounding this magnificent deer, I watched him shake his coat and trot off, out of my life. Dejected, I lowered my bow, climbed down and hiked to the truck.

On the hike down the hill, I felt a bit sad. Another week of hard hunting and I had not shot a single arrow at a deer. But then I reminded myself, hey, you're bowhunting. If you have to

kill something, get a gun. Better to pass up the best buck of your life than risk wounding him. If you're not sure of yourself and your shot, don't shoot. It's that simple.

WHERE TO SHOOT

Arrows are not bullets. They don't kill game with massive amounts of shock. To do their business, they must slice cleanly through hide and muscle, reaching the vital organs of the chest cavity with enough kinetic energy left to cut cleanly through them.

When bowhunting, the only acceptable target is the heart/lung area. Yes, a broadhead-tipped arrow can cause a quick death if it pierces the liver or kidneys or cuts one of the body's large arteries, like the femoral or aorta. But the heart/lung region of the chest offers by far the best and most reliable target. The largest target gives you a bit of leeway in your shot placement. For my money, a double-lung hit is far and away the surest, dead-

Make sure you have a clean shot to the vitals. If not: Let him walk.

Making the Shot on Game

liest shot in all of bowhunting. I've seen tough animals like bull elk and Alaska brown bears weighing more than half a ton hit through both lungs with a razor-sharp broadhead die within 45 seconds, traveling less than 100 yards before piling up. I've seen more than one big-bodied deer and black bear hit the same way run less than 50 yards before going down for the count.

THE *ONLY* SHOTS TO TAKE

How do you ensure your shaft will penetrate both lungs? Simple. *Take only broadside or slightly quartering-away shots and no others.* Ever. These shot angles give you the best chance of making a quick, clean kill: the goal of all ethical bowhunters.

I recently read an article in a hunting magazine penned by a well-known bowhunting authority who told his audience how he had shot a deer that was facing him straight on. Holy mackerel, I thought, I can't believe this guy would take such a shot! The margin for error on such a shot angle is so small as to be almost non-existent. I would never, ever take such a shot. Nor would I shoot a deer facing straight away from me or one that was quartering steeply away. The chances for a poor hit are too great. And I never shoot for the neck or head.

Broadside

On a broadside animal, aim just behind the front leg, about halfway up the chest. If you visualize an imaginary line drawn straight up from the animal's elbow, you can almost see a small crease in the hide. Now draw another imaginary line horizontally through the animal's chest, just a smidgen below the midline. You want to hit him at the intersection of these two crosshairs.

This spot also offers you some leeway. If you hit a bit too far back, you'll hit the liver, which means a quick death. If you hit a bit low, you've drilled the heart. Take care not to shoot too high or too far forward, though. Just forward of this spot lies the shoulder blade, which can stop or severely restrict penetration. Too high and you might actually hit the deer in what we call the dead zone, a section of muscle below the spine

Put the bull's eye right behind the shoulder blade. You have a decent-sized kill zone here.

but above the lungs. If you hit an animal in the dead zone, he might not be severely injured and you possibly won't recover him.

Quartering Away

On a slightly quartering-away angle, draw the same imaginary lines. This time, though, use the animal's opposite leg as your vertical line, with the same midline for the horizontal line. Aiming for the "off" leg will send your shaft through both lungs. But an animal quartering toward you presents a horrible bow shot. The shoulder blade protects the lungs, and your arrow will probably instead wind up in the stomach or intestines, which would be your worst nightmare. Instead, be patient and wait for the animal to turn and present a better shot angle. Most of the time he or she will.

Quartering-away shots actually favor the shooter. Try to put your arrow through the far shoulder.

Controlling "Buck Fever"

The day I quit shaking when a big-game animal comes within bow range would be the day I hang up my quiver for good. I get as excited and nervous today as I did decades ago, to the point of sometimes having consciously to control my feelings to be able to make the shot.

"Buck fever," also known as "target panic," can make us all nervous wrecks to the point of missing even slam-dunk shots at game. It will happen to you too, so don't fight it. Learning to control it is every bit as important as a well-tuned bow, mastering basic shooting skills and accurately judging distance.

You can try a few things to help prepare for buck fever. Concentrate on every practice arrow you shoot as if it were the only shot you'll get all season long. Using a bow set at a draw weight you can easily control helps you to smoothly draw, hold and release when the moment of truth is at hand. Practicing your shooting at a target bale at 10 yards or less with your eyes closed, concentrating only on shooting form, will help ingrain proper shooting techniques and make them an unconscious act when the time comes.

Each individual reacts to buck fever differently. I do several things to minimize it. Once I have decided to shoot an animal, I don't ever look at the antlers or horns again. Instead, I try to focus on the single hair on the chest that I will try to hit with my arrow. I try to predetermine the range to a certain spot, knowing that if the animal reaches that spot it will be, let's say, 20 yards away and I can put my 20-yard pin on my target hair and easily make the shot. I go through a mental checklist before each shot: relax, pick a spot, anchor, sight picture, release, follow through—with the emphasis on the follow-through. In the heat of the moment, for me at least, my excitement wants me to drop my bow arm and watch the arrow hit the animal, which of course will cause me to pull my shot.

The secret to controlling buck fever is first to recognize that you're going to get it, and then, when you do, be able to identify the problem. If you miss a shot because of your excitement—as we all have—recognize the reason, admit it happened and work on controlling your emotions. After all, it is this kind of excitement that makes bowhunting so alluring and rewarding.

And I wouldn't have it any other way.

Learning to control buck fever is an integral part of the hunt. Learn to control it with the ideas outlined here.

Read the animal's posture: If he looks relaxed and unalarmed, he's not expecting trouble. Take the shot.

READING THE ANIMAL'S POSTURE

Another key factor in deciding whether or not to shoot is your ability to read an animal's posture. If he's calm and relaxed, seemingly without a care in the world, this is the kind of animal we want to shoot at! By the time he figures out something's up, it will be too late.

In contrast, a spooky, alert animal can detect the slightest movement you make, even to the point of jumping at the sight of your bow limbs moving forward at the shot. The sound of your bow going off and of your fletching whistling through the air as it races towards them can cause them to jump completely out of the way of your shaft before it ever gets there.

Junping the String

Is "jumping the string" a reality and not a myth? In a word, yes. How so?

Even with a super-high-speed bow-and-arrow setup, the sound of the bow going off and of the approaching shaft cutting through the air will reach the deer long before the arrow ever arrives, at times causing the deer to lunge and "jump the string," which of course can cause a missed shot

or poor hit. The speed of sound is about 1,150 fps, meaning the sound of the bow firing will reach a deer about four times faster than a super-fast hunting shaft traveling 280 fps. And we all know how fast a wired whitetail buck can react to the slightest sound.

This is why many experienced bowhunters—including me—believe in the axiom, "Take the first good shot that presents itself within your comfort zone."

In a nutshell, I worry as much about an animal being too close to me as I do him being too far away. When a deer or other big-game animal gets within 15 to 20 yards of me, it just seems like that critter's internal radar goes on red alert. At that close range they are more apt to pick up the smallest movement, hear the slightest sound or catch my scent than when they are out there 25, 30 or 35 yards away.

To that end, when I set a treestand, I try to set things up so that I'll have a clear shot at an approaching animal between 20 and 30 yards out. I know I can make this shot all day long and I am much more comfortable with the animal out there than at less than 20 yards. By the same token, when I'm stalking an animal out West, I try to creep to within 30 to 40 yards, but I stop there. Under the right conditions, I know I can make shots at that distance, and rather than risk spooking the animal by closing in another 10 yards, I'll go ahead and take the shot or wait right there for it to develop.

SHOOTING UPHILL & DOWNHILL

There will be a different point of impact when you shoot your bow over level ground than when you shoot it at an uphill or downhill angle. How much of a difference depends on a lot of things, the primary influences being the distance to the target, the steepness of the angle and the speed of the arrow.

When you shoot an arrow over level ground, it launches at a slight upward angle relative to the line of sight. Gravity pulls the shaft back down toward the target, causing an arc. If you calculate the distance along the line of sight, shooting at either uphill or downhill angles shortens the horizontal distance to the target. This reduces the amount of time gravity has to affect arrow flight, and the arrow will not fall as far as it would if shot over level ground.

Most bowhunters are concerned with shot angles created by hunting from an elevated treestand. Here's how to make the necessary adjustments.

SHOOTING FROM A TREESTAND

To compensate easily for the downhill effect on your arrow when treestand hunting, practice shooting from a platform that's approximately as high as your hunting stands and set your sight pins accordingly. Here you can do one of two things—either pace off the distance from the base of the tree, setting markers or targets at specific distances, or take a rangefinder reading from the treestand seat. I like to use the rangefinder method simply because when I get to my tree, I don't want to walk all around it and risk leaving a pool of game-spooking human scent. You then set your sight pins to correspond to where your arrows hit.

If practice is impractical and you have to set your sight pins on level ground, four basic things will affect the impact point of your arrow: arrow speed, shot angle, shot distance and how the range is measured.

Realize your angle and shoot a little lower. The closer the target, the less you will have to compensate for a steep angle. This buck is very close, but the angle is very steep. Aim just a little low, if at all, in this particular case.

You can count on the following:

1) Measuring distance from the treestand with a rangefinder will always produce slightly higher hits, simply because the linear distance to the target will be greater than if you paced it off; 2) the higher the stand and shorter the shot, the higher the point of impact, thanks to the steeper shot angle; and 3) the slower your arrow, the higher it will hit, thanks to the higher arc of flight.

For most treestand hunting, the minimal differences in point of impact should not adversely affect your success with game. For example, most treestands are set between 12 and 25 feet high, and shots are generally between 10 and 30 yards. The point-of-impact change between sight pins set on level ground and shots taken from treestands at these distances will be three inches at most for bows shooting arrows at speeds between 180 and 260 fps.

Therefore, if you're shooting under these conditions, you really don't have to worry all that much about the difference in point of impact.

Pendulum Sights & Treestand Hunting

The pendulum sight was developed to help eliminate the problem of compensating for downhill shot angles. This sight features a single horizontal crosswire or pin which pivots on a hinge so that it rises as you take aim closer to the base of your tree and drops as you aim farther away. Combined with a fixed vertical stadia wire, it gives a precise aiming point out to 30 yards or so, the exact distance being directly proportional to arrow speed and the height of the treestand.

This eliminates the need for the treestand hunter to aim high or low to compensate for the varying distance of his quarry from his stand, as well as the tendency to shoot high when using a standard pin-type sight from a high treestand.

Top-quality pendulum bow sights are excellent products and worth investigation by serious treestand hunters. New models feature a fiber-optic sight pin, which aids in seeing the quarry clearly on the cusp of daylight when game tends to be more active. I've used several different pendulum sights over the years with excellent results.

The best advice you can follow is to aim a little low on the chest—more to compensate for the inevitable dropping of the deer as it jumps the string at the shot than for the small difference in point of impact.

THE IMPORTANCE OF SHOOTING FORM

Shooting form can dramatically affect your arrow's point of impact when shot uphill or downhill. The key is to keep your posture the same when taking angled shots as you do when shooting on level ground.

When shooting out of a treestand, it is important to bend at the waist, not the shoulders, when coming down to take aim at your target. Concentrate on keeping a "T" in your upper body created by your arms and torso, which you can do by bending at the waist. Keep muscle tension the same, and don't cock your head so that your sight picture—the angle between your line of sight and arrow shaft—changes.

If you're like me, you'll find that some shooting form changes are inevitable, simply because it isn't always possible to use perfect form under field conditions. Experience has taught me that I tend to shoot a bit high from a treestand, so I compensate accordingly and hold my sight pin a smidgen low.

LONGER DISTANCES, STEEPER ANGLES

Longer shot distances and steeper shot angles will create measurable point-of-impact changes that can cause misses unless you become familiar with how your bow-and-arrow setup shoots under these conditions.

This is especially true in spot-and-stalk hunting out West, where you must estimate range either by using a rangefinder or by eyeballing distance to the target. I've shot some 3-D courses where a 50-yard shot at a target set downhill at a 40-degree angle flew a foot over the target's back. By the way, the same point-of-impact difference is true for uphill angles.

The only formula for success on these types of shots is to practice them diligently. That way you'll learn firsthand how your individual bow-

and-arrow setup performs on these types of shots.

One final note: Don't let the issue of uphill and downhill angles psych you out. Be sure to practice shooting your hunting bow with broadhead-tipped arrows at several different angles, including uphill and downhill, as well as over level ground. Such familiarization will pay huge dividends when it comes time to make the shot.

Practice your downhill shots, watch your arrows and remember how their flight changes.

Making the Shot on Game

Chapter 9

TACTICAL
TREESTANDS

Few accessory items have had as much effect on the growth of bowhunting as the introduction of safe, easy-to-use, affordable treestands. Treestands allow you to hunt above the game, helping alleviate the problems of being seen or smelled. They allow you to get up off the forest floor, where you can see better than at ground level. They also let you wait as a big-game animal turns its body to offer you a high-percentage broadside shot angle.

But treestands can be extremely dangerous. Each year hundreds of careless bowhunters use their stands cavalierly, refuse to wear safety belts or harnesses, throw caution to the wind when stepping in and out of their stands, and don't test their stands before the season to make sure everything is in good working order. Many of these sportsmen and women end up taking nasty falls that result in serious, crippling injuries. Some wind up dead.

You can find several different types of treestands, and within those types, manufacturers offer many different makes, models and accessories. Knowing how and when to use each type can greatly help you become a successful bowhunter. But successfully hunting from a treestand involves much more than buying a new stand, randomly choosing a tree, setting the stand up and climbing aboard. It takes scouting, a knowledge of local game habits and haunts and a willingness to read the woods and make adjustments mid-hunt if necessary. It's a chess game, one of the most interesting and fascinating games a bowhunter can play.

Treestands can be a bowhunter's best friend—or worst nightmare. Learn to use and enjoy them, but never forget that it only takes one careless moment to become a statistic.

BASIC TREESTAND TYPES

longer periods of time. And they allow you to wait patiently for the animal to turn and present a good broadside shot angle. Finally, being above the animal's line of sight greatly minimizes the chances of it seeing you draw the bow and release the arrow. Taken together, these attributes translate into increased success.

Before choosing a treestand for bowhunting, become familiar with the different types and designs on today's market. Each has advantages and disadvantages, depending on where and how it will be used and upon your personal likes and dislikes.

W ith the exception of the development of the compound bow, the introduction of safe, affordable treestands has done as much for the popularity of bowhunting as anything else in the history of the sport.

Treestands have made it possible for the average, everyday bowhunter to, at his or her convenience, locate by scouting a good place in which to ambush whitetail deer—the sport's most important big-game animal—and then wait for the deer to come near.

In bowhunting, the moving hunter, not the stationary one, is at risk. Treestands permit a bowhunter to rise above the game's natural line of sight, hiding from prying eyes. At the same time, they increase the hunter's field of vision by affording a view over and down into woods. This provides a longer timespan to see and evaluate game. Treestands also help get game-spooking human scent up off the forest floor, another huge advantage. Plus, they help the bowhunter remain comfortable, which permits sitting in the woods for

PORTABLE (FIXED-POSITION) STANDS

The most popular stand type, the portable (or fixed-position) stand, features a platform and seat attached by a metal pole, all of which attaches to the tree trunk on top with either chain or nylon webbing and is supported on the bottom by either screw-in T-screws or built-in spikes. You need tree steps or a ladder to climb the tree when using a portable stand.

There are more

Fixed treestand.

different makes, models, sizes and styles of fixed-position stands than any other. The most versatile of stands, fixed-position stands are safe to use in virtually any type, size and height of tree. Many bowhunters like smaller fixed-position stands because they present a smaller outline against the tree trunk than larger stands.

CLIMBING STANDS

Popular in areas with lots of tall, straight trees with few limbs—like oaks and birch trees—climbing stands are designed to be climbed quickly and quietly without tree steps or ladders. They generally have two pieces, with the hunter raising and securing the top piece with his arms, then lifting and securing the bottom piece with his feet. They are usually heavier and bulkier than fixed-position stands.

Climbing treestand.

Climbers are excellent when the hunter is scouting on the move and prepared to set up and hunt hot sign that day. Quick to set up, they allow you to find a tree, assemble the stand and climb into position in a matter of minutes.

This also makes small adjustments in stand location during the hunting day both easy and practical. The downside is that they are impractical to use in trees with lots of large limbs or on trees with crooked trunks. Also, you must remember to connect the bottom section to the top section with a safety rope or cord. If the bottom portion slips off your feet and falls to the ground without the safety cord, you'll be left hanging—literally.

LADDER STANDS

Ladder stands use an aluminum ladder secured to the tree in conjunction with a small, built-in seat/footrest on top of the ladder. The ladder secures to the tree at the top of the stand with a chain or nylon webbing that wraps around the trunk. Usually, a couple of support arms partway up the ladder also secure to the trunk with a small rope or chain. Easy-to-climb ladder stands are most popular on private land where their bulk and weight are not a factor with hunters who leave them set up all season.

Ladder stands are growing in popularity each year because they are easy to set up and are generally very safe. When you begin securing the ladder to the tree, you must make sure that it will not roll off the trunk at the top, a potential problem on small-diameter, slick trunks. Generally, ladders permit you to get only 12 to 14 feet off the ground, with many rising only to 10 feet. They also create a large silhouette against the tree trunk, which deer may spot and avoid.

Ladder treestand.

Tree-Climbing Aids

When using a fixed-position-type stand, you'll need some way to get up and down the tree.

You can buy either screw-in or strap-on tree steps. When using screw-in steps, make sure to screw them tightly into the tree, leaving no gap between step body and tree trunk. Never set the steps so you must reach overly far from one to the next.

Tree steps are available as both solid steps and steps that fold in the middle for compact carrying and storage. You'll also find several footrest sizes. (The larger steps are the easier and safer to use in cold weather while wearing pac-type boots.) The best screw-in steps have long, large-diameter screws that you can bury deep in the tree. On trees with large, thick bark, you might have to chip away the bark to ensure that the step digs into the tree trunk itself and not the crumbly, unstable bark.

Be sure you get to solid wood when screwing in tree steps.

Ladders are gaining popularity because they are quick and relatively quiet to set up, are very safe to climb and cause no damage to the tree. Stand height can be adjusted up as long as you have more sections. When broken down, most ladders can be backpacked easily with a stand into remote areas. When using these portable ladders, I also carry a half-dozen or so screw-in tree steps so that I can get my stand set just so.

You can also buy several types of lightweight aluminum ladders that come in sections, allowing you to adjust height as needed. Most secure to the tree trunk with rope or nylon web straps. They are excellent when used on tall, straight trees. Two basic styles are available: those with sections that are machined to be physically fitted together and those with separate sections that strap to the tree trunk, one over the other. Both work well.

Spikes—similar to a telephone lineman's spikes—are used most often with tree slings and some fixed-position stands. The user attaches one spike to each boot, then uses them to dig into the tree as he climbs with the aid of a climbing belt. Spikes are definitely a graduate-school tool.

Portable ladders are available in a variety of styles. Pictured here: ladder steps (left) and a climbing stick.

Slings

Commonly used with tree steps or "step stix," tree slings permit the hunter to sit in a sling held in place by several nylon web straps and/or rope. Since the hunter remains close to the tree trunk, this reduces his outline and allows him to maneuver quietly around the tree

Bowhunter in a sling.

trunk to change his shot angle according to the direction from which game approaches.

Popular with some bowhunters because of their versatility and the small outline generated against the tree trunk, slings are graduate-level stands that take some getting used to. Most hunters use a pair of screw-in tree steps as footrests once the sling has been set up, which makes waiting in them for extended periods of time more comfortable.

Tripod Stands

Tripod stands are most popular in Texas and portions of the Southwest, where the tall trees needed to support more conventional treestands are few and far between. Tripods are just that—three legs joined at the top, on which a rotating seat or shooting house sits.

Monstrous stands, tripods stick out like a sore thumb unless

Tripod stand.

they are set up inside or adjacent to a small tree like a cedar. If set up and left for a long period of time, though, game generally gets used to their presence. Hunters sitting in a tripod with an exposed seat on top must take great care not to fidget, as they have little or no cover around them. Tripod stands are very stable, very safe and easy to get into and out of. They work well when set overlooking large green fields, feeders (where legal) and open-country water holes.

Homemade Stands

Hunters construct homemade stands with plywood, two-by-fours and four-by-fours, nails and whatever else they have lying around. Use extreme caution when climbing into a homemade stand you're not familiar with; rotting wood and loose steps have caused more than one serious accident. Statistics show that more accidents occur on homemade stands than on any other type.

Homemade stand. Check it often, for safety's sake!

Tactical Treestands

Basic Treestand Hunting Techniques

*U*nder many circumstances, hunting from an elevated treestand can be the most effective method of all for the bowhunter—especially in areas with relatively high game populations, dense cover and terrain that's too flat to permit much glassing. Using treestands safely and effectively is the backbone of whitetail hunting. Treestands are the primary tool in areas where spring black bear hunters employ baiting. And even out West, where spot-and-stalk hunting methods are the cornerstone of bowhunting, more and more archers are discovering the benefits of a strategically placed treestand. However, successful treestand hunting involves much more than simply buying a stand, randomly picking out a tree and climbing aboard. It is a chess game, as much as anything else a dynamic process of move and counter-move where the hunter selects a tree for his stand, gives it a go and then, based on his observations and changes in prevailing conditions, may choose to move the stand to increase his chances at a high-percentage shot.

Improving Your Odds

Scout. You must scout to locate areas where the sign is hot before choosing a stand site. Such areas can include preferred food sources; active trails and trail junctions; funnels; green field edges; fence lines; crops like corn, alfalfa and wheat; scrapes; and rubs. Look for fresh deer droppings, tracks and signs of feeding activity like fresh acorn caps, half-chewed corncobs and places where the ends of browse like honeysuckle have been nibbled on. During the pre-rut and rut, look for fresh rubs and scrapes.

As a general rule, the best stand locations for whitetails cover trails leading from food sources to bedding areas in the mornings and are close to preferred food sources in the afternoons.

Hunt deer, not trees. The right way to look for a place to set a treestand is to scout the woods, find some hot sign, and set up within good shooting range of that sign. The wrong way is to scout, find hot sign, then look for a nearby tree that will accommodate your treestand. That's like the tail wagging the dog. Never forget that the object of the exercise is to get a shot at your quarry. If your stand won't work in a tree within range of the spot you know will produce, it's time to reevaluate both your hunting technique and your stand type.

Watch the wind. Even if you're 20 feet off the ground, you have to hunt with the wind in your favor. Setting up so that game will approach upwind or crosswind of your stand and walking to your stand with the wind in your face are important. For example, when hunting a fresh scrape, it is better to set up 30 to 100 yards downwind of the scrape and not right on it. Just how far depends on the terrain and thickness of the brush. A buck usually approaches a scrape on the downwind side to scent-check it before walking to it; you don't want him coming in downwind of you.

Cover. Contrary to popular opinion, deer do look up! Set your stands so that you have as much cover around you as possible so deer and other game won't spot your movements or your silhouette. You should at least have a backdrop of leaves and branches. With bare trees in late season, set stands in small clumps of trees so the multiple trunks offer cover. When legal, wear camouflage that closely mimics available cover.

Don't trim too much. When pruning branches both around your stand and on the ground to create shooting lanes, take only the minimum amount of foliage to get the job done. Too much pruning will allow the game to spot you before you have a chance to react.

Don't move! Just because you're off the ground and in full camo doesn't mean game won't spot your movements. They will! To control my own fidgeting, I bring a paperback book to read while on stand, and I stick cut branches in the floor of

You want to be where bucks travel.

my stand so game can't see my feet shuffling. The less you move, the more game you'll see.

Beware of hollows. If you set your stand in a hollow, you must be aware that deer might be moving on your level on the adjacent hillsides regardless of how high you set your stand. This makes it easier for them to spot the slightest movement. Generally speaking, I always set my stands either in the very bottom of a hollow or the top of the ridge, but not on a hillside.

Stand height. Choose stand height according to conditions. On flat, open ground, 12 feet may be enough. In thickets, 20 to 25 feet might be necessary for optimum stand placement. Do what's necessary to achieve the optimum compromise between cover, visibility, scent control and your own fear of heights. I personally prefer stands set about 25 feet up, simply because I'm a fidgeter and the added height helps prevent game from seeing me. Also, the added height helps keep my scent floating above game.

Locate trees near deer sign, then make sure you have good sight lines and shooting lanes.

Be quiet! When setting up a stand, traveling to and from the stand site and sitting on stand, unnecessary noise is a red flag to wary game. Secure all rattling stand parts, like chains and exposed metal surfaces, when hauling the stand in. Before the season, lubricate squeaky areas to remove creaks and groans. An old piece of carpet cut to fit makes a warm, quiet foot pad. Take a few extra minutes to take care of details and you'll be more successful.

Lubricate your stand to eliminate unwanted squeaks and creaks that might spook game as you shift your weight.

Minimize your gear. Some hunters aren't comfortable unless they pack the entire Cabela's catalog on stand. Come on, you'll only be there a few hours! The less you bring, the less will get in the way. Everything you need should fit in an average-sized daypack.

Be flexible. If you keep seeing game from your stand but it's out of range, be prepared to move the stand to the area where the game is moving. Why hunt in the middle of the Sahara when you can see an oasis just a stone's throw away? By mid-morning, if there's no action where you are or if the area's been dead for days, climb down and scout for hot sign. When you find it, be prepared to set up and hunt it that afternoon or the next morning.

Ground odor. Game—especially whitetails—will smell where you've walked and will avoid your stand site unless you take great pains to minimize the odor you leave on the ground. Wearing knee-high rubber boots is a huge first step; so is not walking directly on trails on which you think the deer will approach your stand. Do not

Scent-blocking clothing reduces the risk of game smelling you.

touch anything with bare skin, and wash hunting clothes in no-scent detergent, store them in a clean plastic bag and put them on in the field. Showering with no-scent soap before entering the field doesn't hurt. I wear rubber gloves and a cap so my bare hands and hair won't brush up against flora and leave telltale human smell. On stand I usually wear scent-blocking clothing.

The more, the merrier. Like many experienced treestand hunters, I believe that the first time you hunt from a stand is your best chance to shoot an animal from that stand, especially if your goal is a mature buck. So I try to set several different stands each year, hunting specific sites only under perfect conditions. I also love to scout on-the-go with a portable climber or lightweight fixed-position stand, setting it up when I find hot sign and hunting it that afternoon.

Scout from above. In unfamiliar terrain, I like to take a day to set a treestand in an area where

I think I might do some good and that also lets me look over a lot of country. My main purpose is to try to observe game movements in the surrounding countryside. If I see a mature animal I want to hunt off in the distance, I don't hesitate; if the wind's right, I move a stand over to right where I saw him and I start hunting. If he uses the same runway again—and sometimes mature bucks do—I want to be there waiting the next time he wanders by.

Silence is golden. While I have had some success rattling, calling and using decoys while hunting from a treestand, I prefer to slip in and out of my stand like a ghost. I don't ever want the animals to know I was around. However, that's not to say that at the right time, under the right conditions, calling or decoying won't work for a stand hunter.

Prune limbs and branches that will restrict your shooting lanes.

I've grunted up several nice bucks, bleated in a pile of does and smaller bucks and decoyed in some dandy bucks while treestand hunting. Don't be afraid to experiment with these proven techniques.

Use your noggin. The one big advantage we as bowhunters have over the game we pursue is our ability to outthink them. When selecting a specific tree to set your stand in, put on your thinking cap and ask yourself simply, "Why this

Stand height is important. Deer do look up, and you want to get your scent above them too, if possible.

Tactical Treestands

tree?" Have a plan. Anticipate where the game will be traveling and at what angle the stand should be set to your best advantage. Walk a 360-degree circle around the tree before setting the stand. Decide beforehand which branches and limbs to trim. Know which way the prevailing wind is blowing and set the stand on the downwind side of the trails you think the game will use. Know in advance how you will enter and exit the woods to minimize leaving a scent and sound trail that might alert the game.

High treestands allow you to scour the countryside for game movement.

The Waiting Game

In truth, I have a love/hate relationship with treestand hunting. I love the chess game—scouting, trying to figure out what the animals are doing and why, the move and counter-move of finding a prime location, setting a stand and anticipating what might walk by.

On the other hand, I find that sitting in treestands can be as boring as a slow day in church. I was born and raised a spot-and-stalk hunter, and unless I can go get 'em, I get a bad case of the fidgets. More than once, after several days of sitting in a stand I know is in a great spot and not seeing what I'd hoped to see, I've questioned my sanity and sworn off treestands forever.

And then here he comes. The king of the woods in all his splendor. He might be a heavy-horned whitetail buck coming to feed on the freshly dropped acorns, a glossy-coated black bear slipping in to feed on my bait, a mature bull elk ready to roll in a muddy wallow or a dandy muley buck sneaking in for a quick drink at a secret spring tucked away in the wilderness.

In those first few seconds when I see him, my heart tries to beat its way out of my chest, my

palms drip sweat, my composure is shot. My knees will be knocking, my entire body quivering with excitement. Guaranteed!

Whether or not I ever get a shot at him—and many, many times while up in the treestand I've seen the animal I have dreamed about and have not been able to loose an arrow—is immaterial to me. I've won. All the time, effort and sweat equity that went into selecting this particular tree has been worth it. If I am fortunate enough to shoot him, well, to me that's gravy.

I know that using a treestand is the best way for me to get into this position. That's why I continue to hunt from them. It's the same reason you should strive to become a safe and skilled treestand hunter too.

TREESTAND ACCESSORIES

*T*reestand hunters need a select amount of equipment designed to make their days afield comfortable, pleasurable and safe. At the same time, you can't afford to bring everything and the kitchen sink too. There is only so much room up in the stand. You don't want to hang all sorts of gizmos and gadgets in several branches, turning your tree into a sort of high-tech hunter's Christmas tree.

Besides safety equipment like a climbing belt or safety harness, here's what you'll need in order to hunt successfully and safely from treestands.

DAYPACK AND SMALL ACCESSORIES

You need a daypack to carry basic equipment. Keep your pack as small as possible. An oversized pack hanging in the tree will stick out like a sore thumb. You also want to use a pack made from a quiet outer fabric. Polarfleece and Polartuff are the best in terms of quiet; Saddle Cloth is good too. I like daypacks with several outer pockets to hold water bottles and the like. This makes reaching into the pack while I'm on stand quick, easy and quiet. I also prefer packs with outside compression straps that permit me to strap my bulky jacket and overalls to the outside of the pack when hiking to and from my stand.

My daypack always contains basic hunting gear including: a sharp hunting knife; small whetstone; 50 feet of parachute cord; small first aid kit; compact 6-foot, 1/4-inch tape measure; Allen wrench set; fire starter of some type; toilet paper in a Ziploc bag; hunting license or tags in a Ziploc bag, together with written permission to hunt private property; quart of fresh water; lunch or snacks; area maps; and compass with small mirror. Because I wear contact lenses, I always carry some eyedrops and a spare pair of eyeglasses. I attach a spare truck key to an interior pack pocket with a safety pin. I keep a small multi-tool either in my pack or on my

belt. I almost always carry a lightweight, compact rain suit from Whitewater Outdoors in the bottom of my daypack, crammed into a small stuff sack. I keep two heavy-duty plastic garbage bags in the bottom of my pack. And I never, ever head to a treestand without a paperback book to help me pass those long hours between game sightings without going bonkers.

Branch-Trimming Gear

Pruning shears are essential for snipping off small branches and limbs while trimming shooting lanes and clearing an open path to and from the stand. For trimming large branches and limbs, Browning, Uncle Mike's, Game Tracker and Bracklynn Products all make top-quality, lightweight, compact saws.

Rope

You need a pull rope for hauling your weapon and daypack up and down the tree. Nylon parachute cord works well, or you can buy inexpensive pull ropes with plastic clips on the ends from companies like Hunter's Specialties. I usually carry two pull ropes in case I need some extra length or if something happens to one of them (like leaving it in the tree).

Hooks & Holders

Either small hooks that screw into the tree trunk or holders that clamp onto the stand's platform serve as a bow holder to keep the bow handy and your hands free. If you use tree hooks, carry a couple of spares in your pack. They just seem to disappear, if you know what I mean.

Lights On

Better than a flashlight, a headlamp keeps your hands free for climbing up and down the tree in the dark. A small elastic headband with a built-in holder for a mini-flashlight is another option. Always carry a spare bulb and replace your batteries prior to the beginning of the season.

Find Your Way

Flag the trail you take into the stand with flourescent flagging so it is easy to find in the dark. Fluorescent stick-on dots (Bright Eyes are super products of this kind) that glow in the light of a flashlight also work. You can also use flagging during the blood-trailing process.

Analyzing Wind

An unscented talc-filled puff bottle or butane lighter works well as a wind detector to determine wind direction. A windfloater, a small can the size of a can of chewing tobacco but filled with small, super-light "floaters," is a great product. You can toss a floater into the wind and watch it move about on the currents for a long way, giving you a precise read on the nuances of the wind well away from your stand. Tying a piece of thread with a small, downy feather on either a tree branch or the upper limb of your bow will allow you to monitor subtle wind changes constantly.

Substitutes

I never, ever head afield without spare bowhunting gear like a spare release aid or finger tab, face mask and lightweight shooting gloves.

Optics

My optics—my 7X35 binoculars and laser rangefinder—are always in my daypack, where I won't forget them.

Communication

No, I don't really want to talk to anyone else. But I've found that carrying my cell phone or a small walkie-talkie, like the Motorola Talk About or Talk About-Plus, is good insurance against trouble. Forget it's there to enjoy your hunt, but feel good it's there in case you need it. If you get a deer and need help finding it after dark, or (hopefully!) dragging it to the road, you can call your buddies. If you're going to be late, you can call people to keep them from worrying. And, heaven forbid, if you fall or otherwise injure yourself, you can call for help if you're conscious.

Keeping Warm

Depending on the season, you may need to bring along spare clothes such as a spare jacket, stocking cap or heavy gloves. For late-season hunts, a muff that attaches around the waist and in which I can warm my hands without wearing bulky gloves is a great addition to my basic gear. So are small chemical heat packs designed to warm fingers and toes.

Pee Bottle

'Nuff said.

ARE YOU FEELING LUCKY?

*E*very time you use a treestand, ask yourself this question: "Are you feeling lucky?" If you are one of the hundreds of treestand users who refuse to wear a safety belt or harness, you must feel extremely lucky. You're also probably a hunter who is careless when getting in and out of the stand and who refuses to check steps or ladders for ice, mud or other slippery debris that can cause a fall. Each year, dozens of you "lucky" hunters come home severely injured, crippled or dead.

A survey by the Georgia Department of Natural Resources reported that treestand accidents accounted for almost half of all hunting accidents from 1986 to 1993. The report showed that 99 percent of people involved in treestand accidents were not using safety straps. Twelve percent of the victims had safety straps with them but had not been using them at the time of the accident.

Using a safety belt improperly can result in serious injury too. Treestand manufacturers have done drop-test research with dummies dropped just a few feet.

The results are eye-opening.

"Most people aren't aware that for every foot they fall, they multiply their body weight times 17 in terms of the pressure exerted when they hit the end of their belt or harness," explains John Louk, president of Ol' Man Treestands. "That's the reason people improperly using safety belts may not fall to the ground but are still injured or killed

anyway." As a friend told me once, when they used to hang men in the Old West, they only dropped them a body length; that was enough to ensure a broken neck.

The best safety device is a harness, not the lone safety belt often provided with treestands. If you fall while wearing a harness, you'll remain upright, not upside down or sideways, which makes it easier to get yourself back under control. A harness also will distribute the shock load better, minimizing potential internal injuries.

The best harness I've seen in recent years is the Game Tracker line of Camo Safety Harnesses (810-733-6360). These harnesses, built from heavy-duty camouflage nylon webbing, are designed to distribute weight evenly across the upper body. The basic model is designed for hunters weighing up to 225 pounds, but they even have a "Big Man"

Always wear a safety belt or harness. It's a simple—and lifesaving—rule.

The "Lucky 13" Treestand Safety tips

1 Well before opening day, check over your stands carefully, repairing or replacing broken, worn or loose parts.

2 If you've bought a new stand, put it together and learn how to set it up before the season. Test the stand just a foot off the ground until you're confident both in your ability and in the stand itself.

3 Always use a climbing belt when going up or down a tree, and always wear a safety belt or harness or climbing belt, when setting a hanging treestand in a tree.

4 Always attach your safety belt to the tree trunk before stepping out onto a treestand. Never hunt without one.

5 When stepping onto the stand, place your feet in the center of the stand near the tree trunk, never on the stand edges. Make sure the stand is seated firmly on the tree before transferring all your weight onto it.

6 Always raise and lower your bow and gear with a pull rope. Never carry it up and down the tree and never haul it up until you are comfortably settled in your stand with your safety belt attached. Use a pull rope that is longer than you need so you can swing your bow out away from the tree trunk when lowering it. This will prevent you from landing on it should you accidentally fall.

7 Never wear slippery gloves when climbing. Make sure your hands or gloves can firmly grip the tree steps or ladder, especially when the steps are wet or icy. If there is mud or ice on the steps or on your boots, knock it off before climbing.

Wear a climbing belt when going up or down a tree and when setting a stand. Always select straight, healthy trees.

Test your stand before climbing aboard with your full weight.

8 Snug all tree steps securely to the tree trunk or make sure that a ladder is set securely against the trunk before climbing. A few seconds checking this out is cheap insurance against disaster.

9 When climbing up and down the tree, use the "three-point" approach: Always make sure you have three contact points with the tree before proceeding. That means both hands and one foot or both feet and one hand in solid contact with the steps before advancing. Never take a step when holding on with only one hand; never reach with your hand without both feet solidly placed.

10 Never store bulky gear, like a daypack, under the treestand seat, where you might trip over it. Always hang it from a handy branch or hanger.

11 Never use a climbing stand in trees that are canted more than a few degrees from level.

12 Always tell someone exactly where you'll be hunting and when you expect to be back. I often leave a map, marked with both my treestand location and my antici- pated route to and from the tree, at camp or at home with my wife. If my hunting companions or I don't return when we're supposed to and haven't checked in by radio or telephone a couple hours after- wards, our friends will come looking.

13 Take your time, always use common sense and never take unnecessary chances when using a treestand. Always assume that something will go wrong. After all, it is your life.

model for large men with big chests and shoul- ders. These harnesses are comfortable and allow you to maneuver around your stand and shoot your bow with no interference. If you choose to wear a simple belt-type safety device, fasten it up under your arms, not around your waist. If you fall with it around your waist, the pressure of the belt on your soft midsection can rupture internal organs or your diaphragm.

Fasten a safety belt or harness around the tree trunk at head height when you're standing on the stand's platform, not at waist height. Then you can still maneuver to the edge of your stand, but if you do fall you'll drop less than a foot, mini- mizing the load and keeping you in an upright position.

Treestand accidents can happen to the most experienced and safety-conscious bowhunters. My friend Bill Krenz, a former marketing executive with bow manufacturer Hoyt and Bear/Jennings and currently editor of *Inside Archery*, a leading industry trade magazine, is a superb and highly experienced bowhunter. And yet, during the 1998 hunting season, as Bill tells it, "One minute I was starting to climb down out of my stand to retrieve a buck I'd just shot, and the next thing I knew I was on the ground in a bad way."

Bill broke his right arm and suffered some seri- ous bruising but fortunately nothing more critical. Months of physical therapy and more good luck allowed him to recover from his fall, but he told me, "Never, ever again will I treat getting in and out of a treestand, or hunting from one, as any- thing but serious business. What if I had landed on my head?"

I hunt extensively from treestands of all types. But to tell you the truth, they scare me. I know what a bad fall can do to you. That's why when treestand hunting, I move up and down the tree and get in and out of the stand slowly and very deliberately. I think about every step before taking it. I assume the worst. That kind of caution has helped keep me from a bad fall so far. I, for one, don't plan on winding up a statistic on a game department accident survey. Do you?

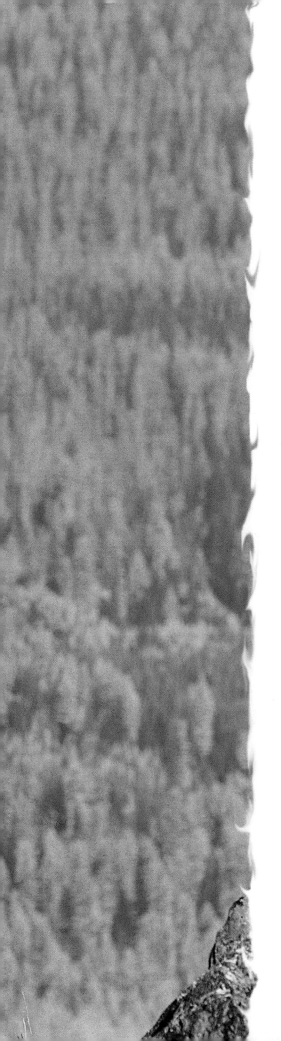

Chapter 10

WESTERN BOWHUNTING BASICS

*I*t was the seventh day of bowhunting somewhere in the Rocky Mountains and I was sore and bone-tired. The sleeping bag was hard to crawl out of, my battered boots tough to pull on. But soon I was sitting atop a rocky outcropping overlooking a large bowl that I could glass along with miles of surrounding countryside. As it started to lighten up to the east, I began glassing and quickly found what I was seeking: a small bunch of velvet-antlered muley bucks.

After I watched them for a couple hours, they bedded down. I planned and executed my stalk. But before I slipped off in pursuit, I took a moment to look around. What a sight! Majestic, pristine wilderness as far as the eye could see. A sunrise of red and orange and purple, soon to become a cobalt sky. The dark timber was pock-marked with meadows, broken up with bunches of colorful wildflowers. Somewhere in the distance a bull elk squealed, feeling the first urges of the rut.

I've been very fortunate in my life. I've had the privilege of hunting on five continents as well as extensively across North America. While every day I spend bowhunting is a special day, none gives me the feeling that days in the vast wilderness of the West do. Every time I hunt the West, I can almost hear the spirits of the early American Indians as well as those of the first white explorers. No wonder they were drawn so strongly to this world! There is no place like it on Earth.

Most average, everyday bowhunters—whitetail hunters—just like you have the means to achieve a do-it-yourself Western bowhunting trip. If you don't have the time to plan your own trip or the equipment to conduct a Western hunt, a number of excellent guides and outfitters will offer to do their best to make your dreams come true. Though a successful Western trip does take planning and research well in advance—but it's nothing you can't handle.

Want to learn more about making your dream of a Western bowhunting adventure a reality? Turn the page and get started. Isn't it time you let your spirit soar like a hawk?

WESTERN BOWHUNTING BASICS

For those who have always dreamed of a Western big-game bowhunting adventure but have yet to venture forth into "God's country," there has never been a better time to take the plunge. With few exceptions, game populations are doing very well throughout the region and hunting opportunities have never been better. Here's what to expect.

ON YOUR OWN OR OUTFITTED?

With its vast tracts of public land, the West was designed for do-it-yourself hunters confident in their bowhunting abilities, physically able to get around the steep, rugged, high-altitude terrain and able to care for their meat once it's down. You can bowhunt species like pronghorn, mule deer, Coues' deer, whitetail deer, black bears and elk successfully on your own.

As demand for available game increases, however, finding superb hunting on public lands without running into a lot of competition from other hunters is becoming more and more difficult, even during archery-only seasons. Knocking on a rancher's door and getting permission to hunt, once a relatively easy thing to do, is getting to be very difficult indeed. Many ranchers have begun leasing their hunting rights to small groups of hunters or outfitters. Others charge trespass fees for access. Who can blame them?

Guided hunts are an excellent option for Western hunting—especially for large animals like elk, where backcountry access via horses or permission to hunt prime private land has become a real key to consistent success. You can find something to tickle your fancy on a guided hunt too.

Want to ride horses into a remote wilderness area and sleep in a tent? Not a problem. Would you prefer a lodge-type environment, with deluxe accommodations and the option to hunt from a vehicle on posted private lands? Lots of options available for that. And you can find just about everything in between too.

A word of caution regarding guided hunting: Not all outfitters are created equal, nor do all outfitters provide the kind of basic hunting experience that will make you happy. Take your time in selecting your outfitter. Make sure he or she has experience guiding bowhunters. Research several options, and have a written contract before any money changes hands.

Here's a look at how hunting for various species stacks up around the West today.

Elk

More elk roam North America today than at any other time in modern history. The top elk-producing states in terms of numbers harvested each year are Colorado and Oregon. The biggest bulls as a percentage of total harvest come from Arizona, New Mexico and Nevada. Idaho, Montana, Utah, Wyoming and Washington also offer some very good elk hunting.

Keep in mind that despite the high elk population, the success rate for public-land elk hunters using firearms throughout the West hovers somewhere between only 18 and 25 percent. For bowhunters that success rate is much, much lower. There may be a lot of elk around, but they certainly are no pushover to hunt!

Mule Deer

In many areas of the West, mule deer numbers are declining due to a number of interrelated factors including the growing elk herds, increased numbers of predators like mountain lions and coyotes, human development on critical winter range and severe winter kill in recent years. However, many areas still offer good hunting and a chance at a whopper buck.

The best overall mule deer hunting occurs in states that tightly control tag distribution and season dates, including Arizona, Utah, Nevada, Wyoming and Idaho (southeastern Idaho only).

Serious mule deer hunters should apply for limited-entry hunts in Nevada, Arizona and Utah.

Yes, Whitetails

White-tailed deer are coming on strong in many areas of the West including eastern Montana, eastern Wyoming, eastern Colorado, northern Idaho, northwestern Montana and eastern Washington. Some Boone and Crockett–class bucks are found each year in these areas.

The Coues' whitetail, the diminutive subspecies found only in the southern portions of Arizona and New Mexico, as well as northern Mexico, is one of my all-time favorite deer to hunt. Generally speaking, populations are strong in the entire range, with the best hunting today happening in the more southern areas of Arizona and along the Arizona–New Mexico border.

Blacktails

Black-tailed deer, the smaller cousins of the mule deer, live along a coastal band from central California north through Oregon and Washington and up into British Columbia. Populations of the

A visit with a landowner may pay off with private exclusive access and maybe some hints on game locations.

It takes patience, persistence and skill—after months of dedicated research—to find, and kill, a big elk like this.

"Pacific Ghost"—so called because these deer of the dense forests are as sly as any whitetail buck—are stable or increasing slightly. The best trophy hunting occurs from central California up through southern Oregon, though good hunting and some big bucks can be taken throughout the deer's range.

Pronghorns

Perhaps the most enjoyable big-game hunt in the West is a trip for pronghorn to states like Wyoming and Montana, where the most pronghorn live and tags are easy to get. But while these states have the most pronghorn, the largest bucks have been coming from limited-tag-draw states like Arizona, New Mexico and Nevada. Colorado, Oregon and California also offer excellent limited-entry pronghorn hunting.

Mountain Lions

With the influx of anti-hunting initiatives that have been passed in recent years targeting the use of dogs and the hunting of the big cats, mountain lion numbers have literally exploded. In states where it's still legal to hunt with dogs—like Montana, Arizona, New Mexico and Utah—hunter success is nearly 100 percent on guided hunts. It does not pay to hunt states where dogs are not allowed, as hunting lions dogless is about as successful as waiting for the prize patrol to show up and make you rich.

Bears

Initiatives have eroded black bear hunting in many Western states, removing spring hunting, the use of hounds and baiting, or combinations thereof. However, bear numbers are high and increasing in all areas. Spring hunting is permitted in Idaho, Montana and Wyoming, with hounds allowed in California, Idaho, Arizona, New Mexico and Utah. You can bait black bears in Idaho, Utah and Wyoming. Colorado and Montana permit no baits or hounds.

Today, the largest bears of all—a surprise to many—are coming from California, where several 600-pounders have been taken in recent years.

Arizona, New Mexico, Idaho, Oregon and Washington also produce whopper bears on a regular basis.

IN THE FIELD

Hunting the West is different, to be sure. But that's what makes it so fun. Here are some details and pointers for success.

Special-Draw Hunts: Best in the West

With increased demand for the available Western big game, more and more states are creating additional limited-entry areas where hunting pressure is low, trophy quality high and access permitted only by drawing a special tag. Without question, these areas offer the best opportunity both for success and bagging a trophy-class animal in the region.

Staying abreast of all the available special-draw trophy hunting areas in the entire West each year is a time-consuming process. States constantly change their programs and application deadlines, and procedures and tag fees can change from year to year. On top of that, the hot areas for trophy-class elk, mule deer, whitetails, pronghorn and other species ebb and flow like the tide. That hot spot of five years ago could be a shopping mall today, something you just can't know unless you track this sort of thing regularly.

To help hunters find out where the best of the best is located in the world of special-draw hunting and to help them wade through the confusing application procedures, several small outfits have begun offering fee services along these lines. These outfits will handle all the paperwork for you and advise you on where to apply for special public-land hunts for various species. The first of these services was the United States Outfitters (USO) Professional Licensing Service, begun in 1990. If you draw a tag through the USO service, you're not required to hire any guides and can hunt on your own if you wish. If you desire guide service, USO can provide it.

"I saw that many of the public-land special-hunt areas around the West were offering the same kind of first-class trophy hunting I was providing on my guided private ranch hunts," explains USO ramrod George Taulman. "It just makes sense for a hunter to apply for these hunts, where he can enjoy that kind of quality hunting for the least expense." For more information, contact George Taulman, United States Outfitters, Professional Licensing Service, P.O. Box 4204, Taos, NM 87571 (phone 800-845-9929). I've used the USO service for many years and have found it well worth the money.

Garth Carter's Hunter's Services offers similar services. Carter, a former state game biologist, helps hunters apply for special-draw hunts and books big game hunts across the continent. You can reach him at P.O. Box 45, Minersville, UT 84752 (phone 801-386-1020).

Scout from above to locate game and be ready to move when the opportunitty presents itself.

Be versatile. Techniques for hunting the West vary greatly. The best Western hunters do not lock into one specific technique but are versatile enough to adapt to the situation at hand. This often means employing several different techniques or variations on a single technique on the same hunting trip, often on the same day.

The West is the home of spot-and-stalk hunting. That means the most successful hunters are those willing to access good vantage points in the dark, then use top-quality binoculars and spotting scopes, letting their eyes do the walking in this big country. However, other techniques also work well at times, depending on the season and the species hunted. For example, calling still draws in lots of elk and can also be an effective and exciting way to lure in black bears. Grunting and rattling work well on whitetails, Coues' deer and even blacktails during the rut, and they will even bring mule deer to you at times. Drives work well for both elk and deer hunters with suitable terrain and enough participants to do it right.

Take enough time. A weekend hunting trip for big game makes no sense for nonresidents who travel long distances and are probably not intimately familiar with the ground they're hunting. My rule of thumb is to take as much time as possible. You can always go home early if you punch your tag. The more days you spend in the field, the better your chances that the animal you've been dreaming about will wander on by.

Choose the right gear. Don't scrimp on equipment and clothing when hunting country that will offer up some of the worst weather imaginable at the drop of a hat.

You and your gear must be ready. Most important are your optics. Use full-size binoculars that gather maximum light during critical dawn and dusk periods and are waterproof and fog-proof. Ditto for spotting scopes.

Carry a quality set of rain gear (I prefer packable Gore-Tex rain suits, like those from Whitewater Outdoors). Buy a good pair of rugged Gore-Tex hunting boots and break them in long before your hunt.

Cutting corners on equipment may seem like good business at the point of purchase, but when your hunt is on the line, the weather's turned sour, the sun has dropped below the horizon and that buck or bull of your dreams is right there, you'll regret every penny you saved when your gear lets you down.

Prepare your body. The most successful Western hunters I've known all my life are people in very good physical condition. That's because it often takes covering lots of high-altitude ground to locate game. Couple that with the fatigue of a week or more of getting up well before the crack of dawn and going to bed well after dark, and you'll understand why the more fit a hunter is the better he or she can continue hunting at maximum efficiency. Get in shape before you go. Period.

Learn to shoot. After a lack of fitness, the complaint I hear most from guides and outfitters is that their clients can't shoot worth a hill of beans. When your dream hunt comes down to one opportunity during the entire week, don't you want to be able to make the shot? Of course you do. That means practicing as much as possible before going hunting. Don't disappoint yourself by being unable to make your one shot count when the time comes.

Nothing in the hunting world rivals Western big-game hunting as a rewarding challenge. I've hunted on five continents. After all that, if I had to choose one place to hunt the rest of my days, it would be the Rocky Mountain West: searching for big bulls, oversized bucks, beautiful pronghorn, sneaky cats and fat black bears. If you try it, you'll see what I mean.

Hunting the West—Information Sources

Alaska Dept. of Fish & Game
P.O. Box 25526
Juneau, AK 99802
(907) 465-4112

Arizona Game & Fish Dept.
2222 W. Greenway Rd.
Phoenix, AZ 85023
(602) 942-3000

California Dept. of Fish & Game
1416 9th St.
Sacramento, CA 94244
(916) 227-2244

Colorado Division of Wildlife
6060 Broadway
Denver, CO 80216
(303) 291-7299

Idaho Dept. of Fish & Game
P.O. Box 25
Boise, ID 83707
(208) 334-3700

Montana Dept. of Fish, Wildlife & Parks
1420 E. Sixth St.
Helena, MT 59620
(406) 444-2535

Nevada Dept. of Wildlife
P.O. Box 10678
Reno, NV 89520
(702) 688-1500

New Mexico Game & Fish Dept.
State Capitol, Villagra Bldg.
Santa Fe, NM 87503
(505) 827-7882

Oregon Dept. of Fish & Wildlife
P.O. Box 59
Portland, OR 97207
(503) 229-5400

Utah Wildlife Division
1596 W. North Temple
Salt Lake City, UT 84116
(801) 538-4700

Washington Dept. of Wildlife
600 Capitol Way N.
Olympia, WA 98501
(206) 753-5700

Wyoming Game & Fish Dept.
5400 Bishop Blvd.
Cheyenne, WY 82206
(307) 777-4600

Hunting the West: Binoculars & How to Use Them

The very best Western big-game hunters spend infinitely more time looking than walking. They do most of this looking through binoculars. In this they're very meticulous, following a well-thought-out game plan. Here's how they do it.

The Right Stuff

Remember only one word here: quality. Buying the best binoculars you can afford is a lifetime investment in increased hunting success. I've never heard a discouraging word from hunters who carry binos from Zeiss, Swarovski, Bausch & Lomb, Leica or Swift. Advanced glassers also know that even though they weigh more, full-sized binoculars with relatively large objective lenses are easier to hold steady, and their larger lenses allow them to see better in dim light at dawn and dusk, when game is most active.

The Tower of Power

There is a wide range of magnification powers available in hunting binoculars. Generally speaking, something between 7X and 10X will do the job. In some very open Western situations, where

glassers look for deer or elk at distances of a mile or more, they use binoculars in the 12X to 20X class. The challenge with binoculars this large is they are harder to hold steady. I have four pairs of high-quality binoculars that get regular use: 7X35, 8X40, 10X40 and 15X60. Which I choose depends on the specific hunt I'm undertaking.

The Grid Pattern

Rather than glass randomly, experts use a grid pattern that covers every square foot of the hunting area. They get comfortable, then begin a slow, sweeping search across the area, drop their glasses, then slowly sweep them back across. Once completed, they do it again. And again. Then one more time. When they're done they know they have not missed a single twig, rock—or deer.

Patience, Persistence

Advanced hunters choose a hunting spot for a reason—they know the game is there, thanks to pre-hunt research, scouting and experience. When glassing, they're in no hurry. They take their time and carefully let their eyes do the walking. Many times I've glassed a hillside and not seen a thing for an hour or more before a deer appears out of nowhere, like some sort of ghost. Patience allowed me to find him.

A Piece of the Action

Anyone can see a deer standing broadside in the sunlight. The best glassers look for pieces of deer—a leg, a horizontal back line in a world of vertical tree trunks and brush stalks, a white rump or throat patch in the dark woods, an antler tine protruding above the brush. I've found deer by seeing a piece of brush that was suspiciously moving faster than neighboring brush in a breeze. Turns out a deer was nibbling or rubbing his antlers on it and came into view only after I looked long and hard.

Sun & Shade

A big-game animal's hide will glow warmly in the sunlight, making it easy to see. But after the sun's up, most critters head for the shade. Your eye is naturally drawn to sunny areas. Make a conscious effort to glass long and hard into dark, shady spots. That's where the deer like to bed down and where they're more likely to be found feeding after dawn.

The Position of the Sun

Whenever possible, set up so you are glassing with the sun at your back or at an angle off one of your shoulders. That means generally facing to the west in the morning and to the east in the afternoon. This does two things: keeps the glare from making it nearly impossible to see through your binoculars and helps shield your body from the prying eyes of game as they look into the sun to find you.

Attack from Above

It is far easier to see into the brush if you're above it looking down than if you're trying to glass through tangled branches and leaves from below. The best glassers climb the mountain or to some other high point in the dark, set up and are ready to begin their search as it begins to get light. In the evening, they stay on station until they can't see, then they hike down to camp in the dark. The cardinal rule: get high but don't skyline yourself. A flashlight is standard equipment for getting around in the dark.

Optical Support

One of the most overlooked keys to glassing effectively is supporting your binoculars. This does two things. First, it steadies your glasses much better than using just your arms. Second, it eliminates user fatigue, which causes the binoculars to wobble and shake ... and your eyes to hurt and head to ache. Standing up and glassing is useless for all except a quick look at a suspicious object. Sitting or lying prone is much better. Resting the glasses on a log or rock will help. Some Western hunters sit behind their pack frames and rest their binos on the top bar. Advanced glassers who scan lots of country for long periods of time or who use binoculars of 10X or more often use a lightweight camera tripod fitted with a special adapter designed to secure their binos on top. This is Cadillac glassing. The Uni-Daptor (602-884-8595) is an excellent tripod-binocular adapter.

Once your glassing work is done, the stalk begins. Be mobile, be flexible, be quiet, use the wind.

Chapter 11

ON THE TRAIL OF BOW-SHOT GAME

You know how the saying goes: "The job's not finished until the paperwork is done." In bowhunting, you can paraphrase it to say, "The hunt's not over until you've found your animal and put your tag on it."

Unless you accidentally hit the animal in the spine or brain, rarely will a bow-shot animal go down immediately. Usually it will run off out of sight. It's then your job to trail it until you have recovered it.

Much of the time, trailing bow-shot game is a snap. The sun's up, the blood trail is big and easy to follow, and the animal hasn't headed into a hellhole thicket, swamp or other horror. Then there are the animals hit marginally that leave a poor blood trail and run into the thick stuff at dark, with rain or snow fast approaching. At that time, you will put your tracking skills and your persistence to the test.

You can learn a lot about a person by working a tough tracking job with him or her. Some hunters will give it half an effort, ready to give up after just a little while. "He's not hit too badly," they'll say. "I'm sure he'll be all right." These people aren't welcome in my camp again. The kind of person I want to bowhunt with knows it is his or her solemn responsibility to do everything possible to find any animal they've hit, regardless of the circumstances. My regular hunting partners and I have an unspoken rule between us. If one of us hits an animal and has trouble finding it, we all pitch in and start searching. If it takes a couple of days away from our time on stand, so be it. This is the most important part of the hunt.

And when it all comes together, when you've put in a long, hard day on the trail crawling on hands and knees looking for pin-drop blood specks and partial tracks and you find that buck, or bull, or doe, or cow ... you feel a joy and pride that's hard to describe. You've done your part as an ethical and responsible bowhunter and shown the animal the ultimate respect. You can hold your head high.

In every sense of the word, you've become a true bowhunter.

ON THE TRAIL OF BOW-SHOT GAME

The sun had just dipped below the horizon and the temperature began to drop. Adrenaline saw to it that the chill didn't get to my bones, though. A good whitetail buck was coming toward my stand, the soft sounds of my grunt tube having pulled him on a string into the hilltop saddle where I had set my treestand. He was a nice 8-pointer, and when he got to within 40 yards and his head went behind a large oak, I came to full draw. At 25 yards he turned and walked left to right with a steady gait right in front of my stand. When he passed through an opening in the brush, I relaxed my fingers and released the arrow. In a blur he raced through the oak leaves and down the hill, out of sight. Soon the only sound I could hear was my heartbeat.

I waited 30 minutes before leaving my treestand, both because it was the accepted follow-up practice where I was hunting and because, with my shaking hands, I didn't feel all that safe unbuckling my safety belt and climbing down. When I got to the spot the deer had been at the shot, I found my bloody arrow but no blood on the ground. I cast out in the direction he'd run but still couldn't find any blood. I must have circled in that spot for 10 minutes before I found one small drop of deep-red blood on a reddish oak leaf.

From there I followed deer tracks until I found the buck about 100 yards down the hill, piled up under a bush. Although my broadhead had centered both his lungs, that buck did not leave any other blood to follow that I could find.

After the Shot

Though you know you've made a perfect shot, the hunt is anything but over at the time of release. Until you've recovered the animal and put your tag on him, you cannot consider it a successful ending. Despite a perfect hit, the animal will probably race off for some distance before falling. In the thick country where most bowhunters arrow game, this means that finding him won't be a sure bet.

Though the adrenaline is rolling through your veins like the proverbial railroad train, there's a lot to do right after the shot. Most important is to watch the animal for as long as possible to see both its posture and where it goes. Carefully noting a definitive landmark at the spot near which he disappears will be very helpful when you take up the trail.

It is also important to stay as quiet as possible. One of the advantages a bow has over a firearm is its silence, which generally does not spook an animal the way the loud report of a firearm will. Don't add to the animal's excitement by making unnecessary noise. Being quiet also helps you follow the animal with your ears. Unless the wind is blowing hard or there's a noisy stream nearby, many times I hear the animal go down before ever leaving my stand.

Get control of yourself. Look at your watch and note the time. My watch has a built-in chronograph, which I click on immediately after the shot so I know exactly how long it's been since the hit. Use your compass to take a reading on the animal's direction of travel from your stand to the last place you see him. This reference can be a big help, especially when hunting from an elevated treestand, as the lay of the land always looks different from ground level.

The Blood Trail

Though I've been bowhunting a long time, I'm still amazed at how many times a well-hit animal leaves little in the way of a blood trail. Some blood trails are so easy to follow that anyone could recover the animal. Other times the trail is

A blanket of snow makes for ideal tracking.

so faint that Columbo would have trouble putting it together.

The Georgia buck described earlier is a good example of a faint trail. Two days later, on that same hunt, I arrowed a deer almost identical in body and antler size to the buck described. The hit was nearly identical too, the broadhead passing through the center of both lungs. The blood trail that deer left looked like it had been made with a fire hose. Even without my glasses I could have followed it at a trot.

Some hits are teasers. Many nonlethal hits, like a hit in the thick muscles of the leg, can result in a lot of blood for the first 25 to 75 yards and then disappear like a wisp of smoke on a strong breeze. The trail may then turn into an occasional drop of blood here and there, leading you on a fruitless tracking job that will last as long as you want to keep it up. Blood volume, while always encouraging, does not definitively indicate a lethal hit.

place until he dies. This means waiting at least overnight on an evening shot and until late afternoon or the next morning on a shot taken in early morning light.

Waiting long enough under these circumstances cannot be emphasized enough. If you spook the animal and he runs another half-mile to a mile before bedding up again, your chances of recovering him drop dramatically. He'll usually leave no blood to speak of, and following tracks is almost always impossible.

This was driven home for me one season on a whitetail hunt in southern Illinois. One morning my buddy hit a young buck quartering away from him and wasn't sure exactly where the arrow had struck. We waited two and a half hours, then took up an obvious blood trail. After two hours and another mile, we found where the deer had been bedded down but obviously bumped by us. We kept after him, following teeny-tiny pinhead drops of blood, often on our hands and knees, at times through a thicket a rabbit would have trouble crawling through. Sometimes it took us 10 minutes or more to find the next blood speck. Finally, after another hour, we found the deer bedded again, and I was able to put a finishing arrow through his chest. The buck had been hit square in the ham. We were lucky to get him.

Of course, all this assumes that weather conditions permit waiting. When it's raining or is threatening to rain or snow, you have to take up the track before Mother Nature washes away all the evidence. A record-book Kentucky 8-point whitetail I shot a couple of years ago is a classic example. The hit looked good, but the drizzle was turning into a light rain, so my buddy Chuck Jones—who was filming the hunt for "Woods & Wetlands"—and I climbed down and followed the deer immediately. He went about 100 yards across the field and into the woods, where he crossed a small creek and headed through the woods toward a distant thicket. We found the buck piled up about 150 yards from the creek. The blood trail was minimal and would have been nonexistent had we waited an hour.

Finding an arrow-hit animal can be challenging, serious work. First steps: look for your arrow, blood and hair.

THE WAIT

For many years, the rule of thumb following a bow shot has been to wait for at least 30 minutes before taking up the track. That's a good rule to follow. Even though the shot looked perfect to you, the animal may have jumped the string without your knowing it, causing the arrow to arrive slightly off-target.

Game that has been hit poorly will generally do one of two things. An animal hit in the paunch area will run off, then move at a slow walk for 100 to 300 yards before lying down. Unless forced from his bed, he'll usually remain in

THE ARROW

On most game, your arrow will pass clean through the animal. The shaft will usually be stuck into the ground or lying very close to the area of the shot. Find it and carefully examine it for blood, hair and other sign that will tell you where the animal has been hit.

The best feeling in the world is to locate an arrow covered with bright red, bubbly blood. This means a lung hit. Very dark red blood can mean a liver or kidney hit but may also mean a leg hit. When this occurs, wait several hours before following. Greenish residue means a paunch hit.

Modern Tracking Aids

Any number of devices on the market are designed to make tracking bow-shot game easier. String trackers are the most popular.

A string tracker, like the Game Tracker 1000, 2500 or 3000 (810-733-6360), Martin Tracer Tracker (509-529-2554) or Saunders On-Line (402-564-7176), have a spool of tracking line attached to the bow's riser and attached to the arrow shaft behind the broadhead with a small barbed tracker tag or clip. When the arrow passes through the animal, the tracker feeds string out. Finding the animal is simply a matter of following the string. Most tracker spools hold between 250 and 300 yards of line.

String trackers are not foolproof. The string can break, the tag or clip can come out of the animal or the line can become entangled in bow accessories or tree limbs and brush. Bows must be sighted in with the tracking device mounted, as adding these parts will change an arrow's point of impact from shots taken without one. String trackers do make quick trailing a reality and are great when the weather's wet. They can also be useful when hunting animals that don't ordinarily leave much of a blood trail, like black bears.

The Game Finder (205-533-5004) hand-held thermal detector utilizes the body heat from the animal to help guide you to it. I had the chance to try one out last spring and was able to track a black bear with little trouble in the thick coastal Alaskan jungle where I had my bait station set.

Following game after dark is tricky at best. A Coleman lantern is much better than a flashlight for picking up blood specks. Coleman also makes a million-candle-power portable spotlight that works even better for this task. Using a mini-flashlight to blood trail after dark is about as effective as trying to convince an animal rightist that a bowhunter is a game population's best friend.

Glow Tracker (906-789-4569)—another after-dark tracking aid—is sprayed in the area where you expect blood to be. The mixture makes blood glow a radiant blue color and works even on seemingly insignificant, hard-to-see spots. The manufacturers claim it will work on blood that is months old or even on blood that has been washed away by rain. I haven't had a chance to try it out yet but am looking forward to giving it a test soon.

Always be ready for a finishing shot when approaching downed game.

Wait as long as conditions allow when this occurs, but at least 12 hours.

Sometimes the arrow shows little evidence of a hit. Look closely and find any sign you can. On game like bears or wild hogs, you may see bits of fat. Smelling the shaft can give you a whiff of marginal paunch hits. Unless I see bubbly blood all over my shaft, broadhead and fletching, I always smell the shaft for confirmation of what the visual signs are telling me.

There will also be times when you can't find the arrow. This does not mean the hit was bad, only that you can't find the shaft. Two instances come to mind. On a whitetail buck I shot low in the chest one October afternoon, the broadhead passed through the pocket on the left side, shot through the center of the heart and stuck into the opposite leg. The deer ran off and piled up after 75 yards with the arrow still in him. He left virtually no blood trail.

A bull elk I shot in New Mexico was above me on the crest of a small knob when I released my arrow. At the shot, he ran out of sight over the crest. After 30 minutes I decided to try to find the shaft to see where I hit him but instead was greeted by a dead elk not 50 yards from the spot of the hit. It took two days to bone and pack the elk out of that hellhole, during which I spent over two hours searching for an arrow shaft I never did find.

On the Trail

Always follow the trail alert and ready for anything. Move along as quietly as you can. I always follow a blood trail as if I were still-hunting the spookiest deer. Try not to spook other animals that may give away your presence to game that is not yet dead. Do not talk loudly, bang equipment or make other unnecessary rattling.

As you follow the trail, mark it with the fluorescent flagging you should always carry in your hunting pack for just such an occasion. Toilet tissue will also work. You don't have to mark every speck of blood, but mark the trail often enough that you can see the last flagged spot.

Look for blood splotches on branches and brush as well as on the ground. Also, watch for tracks, overturned leaves and other sign of an animal passing through the area. I often use a small $1/4$-inch steel tape to measure the animal's track in case I lose the blood trail and have to continue the job by following tracks alone. This helps me identify the target animal if his tracks get mixed up with others.

The best blood trail often ends surprisingly, like a small creek vanishing into the desert floor. When that happens, mark the spot and make a tight circle of 10 to 15 yards as you try to pick it up again. If you find nothing, widen the circle. Use your head. Study the lay of the land and try to guess where the animal might have gone.

While there are no hard and fast rules when tracking game, mortally hit animals will rarely go uphill, though they will often sidehill and climb slight inclines, and they almost always head for the thick stuff. And, on occasion, they will go uphill for a short distance too.

Get down on your hands and knees and look for the tiniest speck of blood on the bottom of a leaf that has been overturned by the animal's hoof. More than once I've picked up the track after losing a good blood trail that petered out by finding a single speck of blood many yards from the last good blood sign.

When the blood trail begins to thin, it's time to use other tracking skills, like following tracks themselves, in combination with intermittent blood specks to help you along the trail. Take care not to obliterate blood sign by walking over it.

If the blood trail ends and you can't find any more sign, start searching for the animal itself. Now's the time to get others to help if they're available. If not, use your compass and map out a grid that you'll walk thoroughly. Leave no stone, log, gully or brush pile unturned as you double- and triple-check all the possibilities. Don't give up until you've either found the animal or are 100 percent sure it's nowhere to be found.

RESOURCES

Where to Find Arrow-Building Products

If you are having trouble finding what you need to roll your own, try the following companies.

Mail-Order Houses
Bowhunter's Discount Warehouse,
(800) 735-2697 or (717) 432-8611
Cabela's archery catalog, (800) 237-4444
Redhead Archery Specialists catalog
(published by Bass Pro Shops), (888) 733-4323

Adhesives
Arizona Archery Enterprises, (520) 772-9887
Bohning Co., (616) 229-4247
Flex-Fletch Products, (651) 426-4882
Saunders Archery Co., (800) 228-1408

Arrow Cutoff Saws
Apple Archery Products, (717) 292-0418
Martin Archery, (509) 529-2554
PAM Archery, (714) 838-8566

Aluminum Arrow Shafts, Raw
Easton Technical Products, (801) 539-1400
Ever True Arrow Co., (770) 684-7298

Arrow Nocks, Point Inserts
Easton Technical Products, (801) 539-1400
Game Tracker, Inc., (810) 733-6360
Saunders Archery, (800) 228-1408

Fletching
Arizona Archery Enterprises, (520) 772-9887
Bi-Delta Vanes, (716) 896-4734
Bohning Co., (616) 229-4247
Easton Technical Products,(801) 539-1400
Flex-Fletch Products, (651) 426-4882
Gateway Feather Co., (520) 805-0863

Fletching Jigs
Arizona Rim Country Products, (800) 635-6899
BPE, (316) 343-3783
Bitzenburger Machine & Tool, (517) 627-8433
Bohning Co., (616) 229-4247
Jo-Jan Sports Equip. Co., (724) 225-5582
L.C. Whiffen Co., (800) 628-6604
Martin Archery, (509) 529-2554
Sky Archery, (314) 731-1600
Sterling Machine, (920) 865-7773

WHERE TO FIND PRACTICE TARGETS

You can generally find an assortment of these target facing products at your local archery pro shop. Delta (319-345-6476) and Morrell Mfg. Inc. (800-582-7438) make a full line of paper-face targets.

Top bag-type targets include the Bracklynn Products Carbon Monster and Dura-Stop (205-345-2697); the Morrell Eternity target line; the McKenzie Targets Tuff Stop target line (888-279-7985); and the Delta Deadstop target line.

Delta, McKenzie Targets and Blueridge (417-451-4438) make top-quality foam targets.

The best broadhead target I've ever used is The Block from Field Logic, Inc. (651-917-3655). The Bracklynn Ice Cube, American Whitetail Foamlite Broadhead Target Targets (812-973-7185), Blueridge Stumper and McKenzie Targets Tuff Block are also good ones.

INDEX